HOLDERNESS ROAD

Through the heart of East Hull

Mary Fowler

Highgate Publications (Beverley) Ltd
1990

British Library Cataloguing in Publication Data

Fowler, Mary
   Holderness Road: through the heart of East Hull.
   1. Humberside. Hull, history
   I. Title
   942.837

ISBN 0-948929-41-3

© Mary Fowler, 1990

ISBN 0 948929 41 3

First Edition, 1990
Reprinted, 1991
Reprinted, 1992

Published by Highgate Publications (Beverley) Ltd.
24 Wylies Road, Beverley, HU17 7AP.
Telephone (0482) 866826

Printed and Typeset by B.A. Press, Tokenspire Park, Hull Road,
Woodmansey, Beverley, HU17 0TB.
Telephone (0482) 882232

Pictures on cover and title page by courtesy Hull Daily Mail.

Foreword

by the Right Worshipful the Lord Mayor of Kingston upon Hull

It is of extreme importance that every aspect of our heritage should be adequately chronicled. I therefore welcome the specific attention which this new publication directs to Holderness Road, an area which has made such an important contribution to our great city.

This major arterial road undoubtedly has an identity of its own and the people who form the local community have consistently demonstrated a strong sense of loyalty to the area. Holderness Road has always been at the heart of the city's development and is historically famous for its mills and for the foundation of other base industries.

East Hull's most famous business, which has achieved international status, is Reckitt's, and the Reckitt family and T. R. Ferens have been influential figures in the social, political and industrial life of the area — and of the city itself.

No single study has been made of this important district since 1903 and Mary Fowler, a long-time resident, who knows it intimately, has decided that it is time Holderness Road and East Hull were brought to the centre of the stage.

In this well-researched book Mary Fowler interweaves her vivid memories of the road with a survey of its long history, with particular emphasis on the 19th and early 20th centuries. The text deals fully with all aspects of industrial, commercial and community development and above all else reminds readers of the people who have been prominent in the story of Holderness Road.

Therefore both as Lord Mayor and as a long-standing resident and local authority representative of Bransholme, it gives me great pleasure to welcome this publication. At last East Hull is receiving the attention it justifiably deserves.

Leslie A. Taylor

Lord Mayor

Blashill's 1865 Panorama of Holderness Road near Southcoates Lane, drawn with some licence in the spacing of the mills. Those not named on the original are: 1. Waddingham's; 2. Marshall's; 3. Bartle; 4. Dale's, Dansom Lane; 5. Hume Street (possibly).

Witham and Holderness Road on Goodwill's map of 1848.

Humberside Leisure Services

HOLDERNESS ROAD

'Round the Town' by Jupiter Junior, from the *Hull Times*, 14 July 1906.
'Until quite lately I was totally unaware that there really was such a place as East Hull. Perhaps I may have been told that there actually did exist a spot of earth (dry land and water) under that name. I may have read it in the paper. But the papers are so bursting full of misleading statements that one is justified in discounting anything they may say. Yesterday I crossed a Bridge. One gets so accustomed to crossing Bridges when one lives in Hull that one scarcely notices it. On crossing this Bridge and asking where I was, I discovered that I had landed on the semi-demi-mythical continent called East Hull. If I had ever given it a passing thought, I had imagined that East Hull was a local flight of fancy, like that child of Mrs. Gamp's conception — Mrs. Harris. So I was in East Hull. The place was not a dream, nor a mis-statement originating in the journalistic mind. I, being somebody, could not be nowhere. And I was in East Hull, therefore East Hull must be somewhere. And here I was. And I was in it. What caps me is how much East Hull has been neglected by its unchristian brethren on the western side of the Bridge. Too many westerners dwell in my recent ignorance. It is nothing to them. Nothing for them. Nothing but a name...'

This hard-pressed piece of ironic journalism was written over 80 years ago, but there are still, in 1990, traces of the feelings it expresses. Hull had expanded beyond all recognition during the lifetime of many who read the above paragraph. A fan-shaped city, its centre was in the old town where the River Hull flows into the Humber estuary, and the struts of the fan were the radial roads. Of these, cutting straight through the mythical area of which Jupiter Junior wrote, was the ancient thoroughfare called Holderness Road. Never a 'romantic' route, its name redolent of battle or history, and lacking picturesque vistas, it was, from the first, a utility, a means whereby people could travel to and from Holderness, and later a place of residence and livelihood for a large portion of the workforce which brought Hull to the position of one of the largest cities in the land and one of the greatest ports of the world. The road is a place of change where challenges have been met and, in some cases, surmounted. To give some idea of the changes in the aspect of Holderness Road and of its use, this book has been compiled.

1

EARLY DAYS

An uncertain track, the origin of the present Holderness Road, existed over 700 years ago, for it is known that the Lord of the Manor of Sutton, Saer or Sayer de Sutton, granted a right of way between Bilton and Drypool to the nuns of Swine some time before 1260. In the charter granted to the town by Edward I in 1299 there was no provision for road links with Holderness, but in 1302, after a Royal Commission headed by William de Carleton and Geoffrey de Hothum, a road out of Hull from the position of the much later North Bridge was designated as the King's Highway. It went through Drypool, Southcoates and part of Sutton as far as Bilton Bridge, which is approximately the place where in 1990 the petrol filling station on Holderness High Road is now situated, or, for those with longer memories, at Rawson's farm beyond the Saltshouse Road junction and where also, earlier this century before road improvements, there was a slight bend and also a hump in the road with Bilton Drain culverted underneath.

This King's Highway, a 40-foot-wide right of way, was more or less on the line of the modern Holderness Road and eventually linked Hull with Hedon *via* Preston. It was a roundabout way, but in the early days somewhat more practicable than a direct route to Hedon along the Humber foreshore which was subject to tidal incursion. Even so, the road into Holderness was frequently impassable due to heavy rain or snow and, although maintenance was in the care of the parishes through which it went, there were many times when it was so totally swamped that, even if horse and foot passengers could just manage to get through, farm produce could not be brought into the town in any quantity. For example: in 1577 the Corporation of Hull stockpiled corn because of the bad state of the road; at some time in the 17th century the inhabitants of Sutton and Drypool made a collection for the repair of the Holderness Road as far as Sutton Ings Gate (now Ings Road corner) following flood damage; and during the great floods of 1764 all the area from Hull to Bilton was under water from 6 January to 1 April. 1764 was an exceptional year; there had been almost continual rains for much of 1763 and the early months of 1764 and many parts of Europe were affected, none more so, it would seem, than Holderness. By then Holderness Road was turnpiked but the toll houses were deserted that year as no travellers could pass, except possibly by boat, and it is recorded that one man who tried to get through with horse and boat was drowned. Even as late as my 1930s childhood, the sight of flooded fields around what is now Grasby Road was common in winter and by then, of course, drainage channels (sporadically excavated across the area for many years) included a deep ditch along the north side of Holderness Road from No. 893 to the Four-in-Hand, with other ditches at right angles to the road, bringing water down from a higher level near Sutton.

The land across which the early Holderness Road passed included an extensive area called Summergangs Common. The name was variably spelled and in Sheahan and Whellan's *History of the East Riding* (1856) the following derivation was given: Somergangs — a contraction of South mere gangs or pasturage, the second syllable, mer, from its being level and subject to the overflowing of the surrounding water. In simple terms, it was where the sheep could gang (go) in summer but not in winter. Broadly speaking, Summergangs was in two fairly distinct areas, both straddling the main road. Nearer the town, a roughly rectangular area had the road as a diagonal, so that, from Dansom Lane to the present Durham Street or thereabouts, would be open pasturage, the roughly north-south eastern boundary being a stream that crossed the road and turned, petering out in the Growths (Groves) of Drypool beside the Humber. The other area was further out along the road and more irregular in shape, a great semicircle bounded by the curving Summergangs Dyke and Holderness Road from, say, Durham Street to Ings Road with a part south of the main road from Mile House to Maybury Road. The two areas of the Common were adjacent with streams in between them.

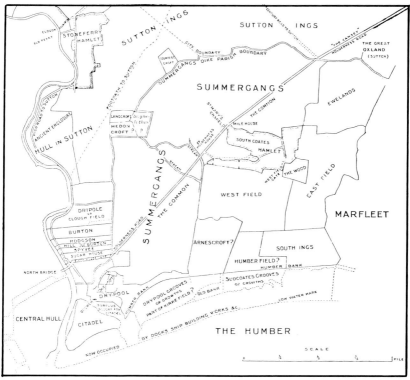

Map of East Hull, derived from Thomas Blashill's Key Map, showing old field names, the extent of Summergangs Common, etc.

3

From Dansom Lane corner to Ings Road the road passed through Drypool parish, including the old township of Southcoates. Beyond Ings Road it was in the parish of Sutton until Bilton was reached. The name Somergangs or Summergangs, as a district, persisted well into the 19th century, and, when the area was sparsely populated, addresses given in directories could be merely 'Somergangs', even for properties as much as a mile apart.

Old maps show the start of a road from an earlier North Bridge crossing the river a little way downstream from today's bridge. In medieval times the river was crossed by a ferry a little way to the north of the modern Drypool Bridge; then, as part of or adjunct to Henry VIII's Citadel of 1541, a North Bridge of six arches was built; in 1785 this was replaced by another of four arches and central drawbridge, from a design by John Smeaton, a bridge which was repaired and altered in 1832; and the next, a horizontal drawbridge designed by Martin Samuelson in 1870, was at the position indicated now by the two metal studs or bollards, which, being on the remaining bit of roadway about 30 yards south of the present bridge, is a good viewpoint to look at North Bridge or to see it open and close. Martin Samuelson's bridge is remembered by many, as today's North Bridge was opened on 10 August 1931. The trams, as I dimly remember, used to lurch round the curve from George Street to the bridge approach and again rolled round the corner from the road in front of Annison's on to Witham. This bit of road was for more than 100 years, during the 18th century and at least until the 1850s, called Bridge Foot and marks the limit of the Citadel.

On Hargrave's map of 1791 the Road to Headon [sic] from North Bridge curves round the remains of the Citadel's North Blockhouse (which was there, latterly as warehousing, until 1801-2) and straightens into what is now Witham but was formerly Blockhouse Lane. Mountain's map of 1817 gives the name Witham, a wide road even then, and shows Holderness Road starting half way down. The town map in *Cragg's Directory* for 1835 had Holderness Road starting at the junction of Witham and Oldbourne Street — the latter a printer's or cartographer's error for Holborn Street. As Clarence Street was not cut through to Holderness Road until 1902, the main road turned from Witham on to Holderness Road proper as it does now, but the open triangle now occupied by the roadway in front of the Windmill Hotel was filled with cottages and places of work. Mountain's 1817 map had Blockhouse Lane also for the street running south from the main road past the Windmill Inn and the (then) Tinegate's mill adjacent to it, but in 1842 Goodwill and Lawson's map shows Witham as today, with Albion Place and Naylor's Row in place of the 1817 Blockhouse Lane. As Fitch and Nailer had a mill 'near Witham' in the 1790s and into the 1800s (the name becoming *Naylor* in *Battle's Directory* of 1803) I think this is the origin of the name which came into use about 1820. Addresses in the middle

4

of last century had 'Holderness Road' for the eastern end of what is Witham today; this included the area round the great Wesleyan chapel — Kingston Terrace, Holborn Mount *etc*. When Clarence Street was cut through and the old property swept away, the junction became a skew crossroads with Dansom Lane: Windmill Corner to everybody who knows East Hull. The buildings near Blyth Street, next to the former Gas Showrooms, were built after the Clarence Street development and the sign on them for Holderness Road is much later in date than the other 'Holderness Road' at the corner of Dansom Lane, on buildings which have been there since about 1850. Both signs, however, mark the beginning of Holderness Road as it is at the present time.

Two major changes took place in the 18th century which brought Holderness Road closer to its present form. One was the enclosure of the ancient common lands; the other was the establishment of turnpike trusts to maintain the roads by means of tolls.

In 1745 a turnpike road was established to link Hull with Hedon *via* Preston. Tolls were extracted from travellers at certain points, the money being intended for the upkeep of the road. It was directed by the Act of 1745 that there should be a bar at 'Somergangs Gate next adjoining Sutton Ings', *i.e.* at Ings Road corner. This is called the Holderness Turnpike Bar in some of the directories where the toll-keepers' names are given. For example, in

Wyton Bar. The Toll House as it was in the 1880s.

5

1814 the toll-keeper was Joseph Myers, in 1815 the Widow Woodmansey, and in the 1851 census return two separate entries for the toll bar list the households of William Dawson and William Sharp. This had to be the first bar going out of Hull and the second was to be somewhere between Somergangs Gate and Sacred Gate in Hedon. The toll-house was built at Wyton Holmes; the fork of the road from Hull to Sproatley and Preston is still called Wyton Bar and, although the toll-house itself was demolished soon after World War Two, the Victorian house at the other side of the road survives, much altered, at the garage. In the early days of the turnpike, a coach drawn by six horses was charged a shilling (5p) at the Somergangs Bar and sixpence (2½p) at Wyton, but this was before it was realised that different effects were produced on the loose surface by wheels of different widths, and tolls were adjusted so that vehicles doing more damage to the road were charged at a higher rate.

Where there was a turnpike road there were mileposts. The first one from town, measuring from North Bridge, is lost, but was marked on the 1888/9 Ordnance Survey at the corner of Henry Hodge's garden at Ivy House, almost exactly opposite the remaining old portion of Brunswick Chapel. However, the Crown Inn is often called Mile House by a true East Hull person, and the area around the Crown, with a farm next to it and farms *etc.* across the road, was called Mile House on many maps of the last century, although some of them reserve the name for Galloway's farm next to the inn. But a mile from where? The Crown Inn is not an exact mile, or anywhere near it, from North Bridge, Windmill Corner or Ings Road. It is not even an exact mile, but a little more than that, from the Four-in-Hand, but is it possible that in days gone by it was 'near enough' for a traveller to say as he left one inn that it was a mile to the next? Curiously enough, Mile House is almost exactly equidistant as the crow flies from Sutton and Drypool churches, but the distance is much more than a mile. Thomas Blashill in his *Evidences Relating to East Hull* makes the suggestion that the ancient chapel of St. Mary may have been near Mile House 'where Holderness Road turns as if to avoid some pre-existing obstacle'. Was this a meeting-place of some significance?

'Hull 2 miles' is marked on a stone set into the wall between the shops at Ings Road. This has become known as Carrick's corner because there has been a shop of that name there since the 1920s. When the buildings were refurbished in the 1960s a newly-inscribed stone was put into the wall in place of a worn one that had been there for many years, a nice reminder that this was the position of the toll-keeper's house at the Somergangs Gate.

Just beyond the Diadem Grove roundabout is a mounting stone milepost, replaced in roughly its former position when the dual carriageway was extended in the mid-1950s. In the 1930s the stone was on the bank of a deep and narrow ditch, part of Bilton Drain, remarkable in my memory for the lush growth of meadowsweet in high summer. This stone must have been previously moved, as the 1853 Ordnance Survey shows a milepost set not in that position but on the north side of the road outside Eastfield Lodge, quite a distance on the Hull side of Saltshouse Road. There was a metal horse-trough near the Saltshouse Road junction, as I remember, and a seat, but the milestone was on the south side in the 1930s and 40s, as described. The incised wording was 'To Hull 3 Miles'. 'To Hull' can only just be deciphered in a picture of 1969, but the decay has accelerated, no doubt because of fumes from passing traffic, and it requires imagination now to see more than 'Hul' *[sic]*.

The four-mile post is on the south side of the road beyond the Asda store. Replaced after the last war, it is a metal plate cast by W. Smith and Sons, Grove Works, Barnard Castle, fastened to a concrete block. Perhaps the plate is pre-war and, as the only reasonably legible milepost on this road outside the then city boundary, was removed at the outbreak of war in case of invasion.

By now we are beyond Holderness Road proper but still on the turnpike, so it is appropriate to mention the mounting block at Wyton Bar and the six-mile stone some-way beyond the farm called Preston Field; also to remember another amenity of a main road for carriers and others, the well for watering horses at the junction of the road to Lelley (Watthering *[sic]* Well Lane).

The turnpike trusts ceased to function in the 19th century with a gradual turnover to the parish and then to the town authorities, the Hull-Preston-Hedon Trust being wound up in 1878. No doubt there were acts of private charity supplementing any formal maintenance, if only in the form of rubble put down near owners' or tenants' gateways in bad weather.

Holderness Road was one of the roads which made a framework upon which the town expanded radially during the last century, in some areas more quickly than others. An easterly road direct to Hedon was suggested in 1830 and established in the next year or two. In 1835 an agreement was reached that the turnpike trusts' responsibilities should be taken over by a local rate within the area when a continuous line of houses along the road was completed. In 1832 the ancient boundaries of Hull were altered when a new parliamentary borough was created and later that decade, in 1836, the municipal borough was made to coincide with the parliamentary one. There was major extension of the town to the east of the River Hull and the Somergangs Gate became the boundary on Holderness Road, about two miles from North Bridge.

An important result of the enclosures of the 18th century was increased activity in the matter of drainage of these low-lying lands. The Act of enclosure was authorised in 1763 and the awards or allotments of lands to individuals made five years later, although some private agreements had already been made. Blashill in his *Evidences Relating to East Hull* wrote that he believed that until this time Holderness Road was open to Summergangs

Common, but that ditches were cut to define the boundaries of the new fields once the awards of land were made under the Act. The effect could only have been beneficial. Even though the channels may have been rather haphazard, as much for boundaries as for drainage, earlier natural watercourses were nevertheless used as boundaries and, once the allotments or allocations were settled, landowners created fields surrounded by ditches and hedgerows. The road, too, was therefore defined and no longer was it possible to make detours on common land to avoid boggy or rutted patches.

Any drainage channels which were cut in the early centuries of the existence of Holderness Road were meant for a prime purpose: to take surplus water away and leave land less boggy and marshy. However, some were big enough to have been used by small boats and some were a useful source of fish and eels. Bilton Drain, for example, I remember as a sizeable ditch in the 1930s. It formed the boundary between Sutton and Bilton at Ganstead, crossed the main road as described earlier, and then took a more southerly course. Until the building of Bilton Grange Estate it flowed (sluggishly) along the side of the southerly stretch of 'old' Marfleet Lane, carrying water all year unless the summer was excessively hot and dry, before disappearing under the road and discharging into Holderness Drain at Bilton Clough near Maybury Road. Part of another old watercourse, the Summergangs Dyke, was in the 1930s a tiny shallow ditch in the playing fields of Maybury Road School, curving and running behind houses on Holderness Road, then culverted diagonally under the crossroads to re-appear and form the boundary between East Park and the even-numbered houses of Ings Road, just as it had formed the old town boundary. Tracing these ditches on old maps gives the clue to their antiquity; some, including the Summergangs Dyke, obviously pre-dated the cutting of the Holderness Drain, by far the largest channel to cross Holderness Road, and created as a proper drainage channel from an originally natural stream, the River Wilflete, about 1832.

The term King's Highway has more significance hereabouts than in some other places. The road, through the centuries, had to provide a causeway above the open common where the sheep grazed the often wet ground. The name Holderness High Road persists for the stretch beyond Ings Road and, until it was updated and improved, the turn off the main road on to Marfleet Lane had an appreciable downward gradient. My mother, born 1893, often used the term King's Highway for Holderness Road. She was brought up in Keyingham and spoke of the many tramps who would walk miles for a night's lodging at Patrington Workhouse, the price a shift of stone-breaking, to make stones small enough to fill holes in the road. Boots, said my mother, were essential in her childhood, for the roads were often rough, with loose stones bigger than the chippings used today. The road through Keyingham was the turnpike continuation of Holderness Road from Sacred Gate in Hedon to Patrington.

One has only to look at Holderness House to realise the importance of a small rise above the surroundings. This house was one of few dwellings built along the road before the middle of the 19th century. The second house on the site, it stands in land allotted to Mr William Constable at the enclosure. A house called Summergangs House was first built there and occupied by Mr Thomas Hall. From April to October 1785 it was advertised in the *York Courant* each week as 'A handsome new-built Mansion-House commanding a beautiful and extensive view of the River Humber'. It passed into the ownership of John Kirby Picard who added a semi-circular porch and front balconies, then to John Broadley and eventually to the Jalland brothers, who, in 1838, pulled it down and built the present house on the site. It occurred to me, when walking up the considerable flight of steps to the front door to visit a friend there, that perhaps the Jallands built this house on the rubble of the old. By 1838 little had intervened to break the fine view of the estuary, but no doubt the Jallands expected far-reaching changes in East Hull as the new municipal borough was then two years old and the new direct road to Hedon had been open about five years. However, Holderness Road was still a country lane or worse in our terms, the land around low-lying, and to build a house on a mound was a wise precaution, not merely a conceit for its appearance and its view.

The disposition and sometimes the names of the streets off Holderness Road and its hinterland were very much affected by the areas of land allotted to various individuals at the enclosure, as these parcels of land were in their turn affected in some measure by the shapes of the ancient fields and commons. During the years just after the enclosure awards and into the 19th century, some landowners acquired large areas of land by dealings in the original allotments and by the middle of last century the whole of the district was in the hands of comparatively few people. For example, Henry Broadley, M.P. for the East Riding of Yorkshire, owned a large, irregularly-shaped tract of land, one side of which abutted the main road roughly from where Balfour Street now is to somewhere near Southcoates Lane. This was sold off for building, piece by piece, over a very long period of time, New Bridge Road later slicing pretty well through the middle of the original area. The fields bordering Holderness Road were relatively narrow; the shorter ones were near Southcoates Lane and they became progressively longer nearer the town. Streets which were built here, Morrill Street and Craven Street (the latter named after Dr. Robert Martin Craven, the mid-century owner of the land) were cut parallel to the old field boundaries and thus Morrill Street, Sherburn Street, *etc.*, were shorter than Arundel and Craven Streets. The even older north/south field boundary between Southcoates West Field and Southcoates South Ings, nearer to Holderness Road — both these fields pre-dated the enclosure — can be lined up from three points on a modern map: the bottom of Dene Street, the bottom of Jesmond Gardens and the bend in Morrill Street. New Bridge Road was cut through in a line that would give back gardens which abutted this old boundary to the houses first built on the west side of the road, so New Bridge Road is not on the boundary itself. At the other side of Holderness Road, land was held by the Rev. John Courtney and John Nornabell, giving names to two of the streets there. These streets were also perpendicular to the main road, just as the old field divisions had been.

MILLING, above all else, dominated the industry on Holderness Road in the 19th century as the mills themselves dominated the skyline. From Dansom Lane onwards, 11 mills were on the main road in the next mile and a half, ten of them in the early part of the century with sails, although chimneys would be added near some of them later as the owners turned to steam power. These were the Holderness Road landmarks; there were no steeples nor church towers to be seen, except Preston and Hedon in the far distance and the more elevated village of Sutton with its church and windmill to the north, and after 1844, St. Mark's in the Groves. Certain ancillary, yet independent, works began to develop in the mid-century. For example, by 1861, Thomas D. Barker was in business at the rope works which had been in existence at least ten years before that. Also the beginnings of the Hope Iron Works were there when Edward Boyd set up as millwright in 1867. In 1914 the Hope Iron Works advertised as 'Makers of cement mill machinery: crushers, washmills, slurry pumps, elevators and conveyors. Makers of paint mill machinery: granite rollers, mixers, cone mills' — showing that their trade had diversified to meet the needs of the changing types of milling carried on in Hull in the intervening years.

The corn and seed millers were part of an agricultural past. As technology changed by the introduction of steam power and the use of rollers instead of stones, as the national economy fluctuated and competitive imported flours affected their trade, so the millers had either to adapt or to fail in the commercial race. Corn milling for flour predominated on Holderness Road, but there were millers of mustard, linseed, rapeseed, *etc.* in business at various times.

Some family names re-appear time and time again among the millers of Holderness Road, as the milling community formed partnerships and working relationships and there were inter-marriages among the families in the district and in the East Riding. A number of them had come to Hull from Lincolnshire or from the villages of Holderness, but, once settled in business, the families stayed in the Holderness Road area for many years.

Many more millers' names are in the directories and census returns than the number of mills along the road, but some are of young apprentices only twelve years old and others are of workers, neither owners nor tenants of particular mills. Because of the vagueness of addresses given also, it is impossible to match all the workers' names with the mills, but the jigsaw

pieces afforded by the various directories and census returns yields the following picture of **HOLDERNESS ROAD MILLS.**
1. **Blockhouse Mill.** Opposite Dansom Lane, in line with the centre of Witham, it was a four-sail windmill with extensive outbuildings. It is depicted on Jefferys' map of 1775, and so, in 1790 when Robert Stickney was the miller, the substantial tower mill had most likely been built for some time, but maps drawn for the enclosure show only a small wooden mill. It was an established concern when it was shown as Thompson's mill on Anderson's map of 1814, for in 1812 it had been converted into a Stamper press mill for vegetable oils and worked at least from 1800 to 1831 by Robert Stickney Thompson. In 1838 James Rook (or Rookes) was the miller, some time later Samuel George Kidd, and then in the '60s and '70s Benjamin Pickering, who often rented it out to other millers. It continued as a seed-crushing mill until 1904; the premises were then used as an animal food factory by Wray, Sanderson & Co. until 1947 when the firm was taken over by the Premier Oil Co. The cobbled entrance yard to the mill is still there (1990) between Nos. 16 and 20 Holderness Road. Jackman's flax carding mill, also wind-powered, was behind the Blockhouse mill in the early 1800s fronting Starch House Lane, later Blyth Street. The earlier name of this little street reflects the fact that Robert Thompson was a starch maker as well as a miller.

Tinegate's mill beside the old Windmill Inn.

(Picture courtesy of Mr. H. L. Thompson)

11

2. **Marshall's Mill** is on Anderson's map of 1814 as a five-sailer approximately where Denmark Avenue would later be, that is, opposite the present Green Man public house. J. & W. Marshall were milling on Holderness Road by 1810 although the family firm had been established in Garden Cottage Row, Myton, long before that. William Marshall continued at the Holderness Road mill until at least 1835, by which time he was 60 years old and in 1851 was living in a newly built house in front of the mill. Since George Priestley, corn miller, was his next-door neighbour, I assume that Priestley was working at the mill as Marshall's tenant or manager. William Marshall was in the same house in 1858, but by 1861 the miller was definitely John Edward Tinegate, employing one man — John Wreghit Rank, wheelwright turned miller, son of John Rank. At the 1871 census it was called the Steam Flour Mill, and Thomas D. Rowntree was there later that decade. The mill is shown on Peck's map of 1882, but, as there are no directory entries associated with it and as Denmark Avenue was built soon after, the mill must have ceased to function about that time.

3. **Bartle Windmill,** a four-sail corn mill, was between the later Kent and Beeton Streets. Called Bird's mill in 1814, it was worked by John Bird from 1806 to 1818 and probably longer. John Bartle was a baker at 49 Whitefriargate in 1823, but had added the mill to his enterprises by 1831. Who had it in the 1840s is not clear, but the following advertisement in the *Eastern Counties Herald*, 28 May 1840, indicates that the mill was by that time held by the son, William Bartle, and also gives an idea when a further change of tenant occurred:

'TO BE LET, the Wind Corn Mill situate on the Holderness Road, occupied by Mr. William R. Bartle, with the drying mills, granary and six tenements thereto adjoining. Further particulars may be known by applying on the premises.'

Richard Wilson was foreman at the mill in 1851, John Edwin Tinegate and John Stephenson were millers successively during the 1850s and '60s and soon after it was taken over by Richard Topham Kirby, originally from Weaverthorpe, who had considerable milling interests — in Wilmington and at the Bell Mills, Driffield, where he lived. By 1874, when Kirby was in his early thirties and had had a few years' interest in this mill, it was abandoned and demolished before Pettingell drew his pictorial map of Hull in 1881. Pettingell depicted a row of three-storey shops/dwellings in front of the mill yard, Leonard's Buildings, which I imagine were typical of the time, flush to the pavement and similar to the ones remaining opposite near Brazil Street. In 1853 the site was extensive, as shown on the Ordnance Survey; then it was Bartle Yard, the mill well back from the road, with a pump, corn seed kiln and gardens. From the time of the mill's demise, an open space existed called Kirby's Mill Yard for a few years and then Old Mill Yard up to the last war. By 1889, as Old Mill Yard, it housed several businesses, among them Joseph Ward, joiner, a firm which extended to become 'joiner, builder and undertaker', and which was there until between the wars and as a building firm contributed a significant number of houses to the Holderness Road scene, including No. 853, The Briers, which Ward built for himself in 1912. In my recollection of the 1930s and post-war period, single-storey shops blocked all but a yard entrance at the Bartle Mill site; these were occupied by Needham's fireplace showroom and Bob Sewell's greengrocery among others, with M. Rock's sweets and tobacco shop, a two-storey building, set forward at the Beeton Street end of the row. Bombing took the Southcoates Station Hotel from the corner of the street.

4. **The Holderness Steam Mill** was at the corner of what became Abbey Street; eventually the Withernsea line ran quite close to it. From at least 1831 Thomas Petchell & Co. were corn and commission agents with a counting house or office in Scale Lane and either works or a residence in Summergangs. As the Holderness Steam Mill was built for Thomas Petchell in 1838, this earlier interest in the business gives a hint that there could possibly have been a windmill on the site before. However, this was a steam mill from the first, built in two blocks, an engine house (which had the single-storey premises of Boddy's, undertakers, in front of it in later years) and a lower, longer building for the mill itself. It is this latter section that survives and is now being converted into an hotel. Between 1848 and 1851 the mill was taken over by the brothers Alfred and Edward Henry West, becoming known as West's corn and linseed mill and continuing thus for about 50 years. The West brothers were the sons of Leonard West, grocer and tea dealer in Silver Street and also brick and tile maker in Summergangs, his home being Summergangs Cottage, near where St. Columba's Church is now situated in Laburnum Avenue. Edward Henry, perhaps only a sleeping partner in the milling business, lived at Summergangs Cottage with his widowed mother Ann West, for many years, but Alfred was close to his work at Holborn Cottage behind the mill and adjacent to the railway line. Alfred West rented out the mill, using it himself with one tenant, or let to two tenants at the same time. In the early 1860s, for example, Charles Rook was at the steam mill employing five men, in the '70s Thomas D. Richmond was flour milling there, and ten years on the premises were shared by Richmond and Joseph Rank, each having a few days of the week. Rank continued renting from West until his own new roller mill, the Alexandra, was opened in Williamson Street in 1885. In the late 1880s Richard Marshall was using the mill, about which time Alfred West left Holborn Cottage for Summergangs, presumably in retirement, although the mill remained in his name into this century. For many years, until 1988, it was Needham's fireplace factory, the front building which had housed the engine having been demolished in the 1970s.

5. **The Six-Sailer,** a corn mill, was well back from the road, opposite what is now the Craven Park public house. This mill and the Blockhouse

were the only mills on Jefferys' map of 1775 on Holderness Road. At one time it was said that its sails began to turn in the opposite direction after a man had been killed by them. The supernatural element of this bit of East Hull folklore was scotched by Thomas Blashill when he quoted John Ellam, Vicar of Drypool, 1863-1876, as saying that, the accident having happened during the mill's construction, the owner had the sails reversed as a mark of his sorrow. I do not know who the original owner was, but Richard Ouston from Newland was the miller there in 1838 and Thomas Wreghit, John Rank's brother-in-law, from at least 1851 to 1872. I do not think milling continued there very long after that, although a mill tower is marked on Peck's map in 1882; certainly the building was removed before the end of the century. As at the Bartle mill, other businesses used the yard in later times, and in the yard of the six-sailer in the 1870s were the premises of Alfred Wright, cod liver oil manufacturer.

6. The 'Anti-Mill', roughly where Presto supermarket now is, was built in the 18th century and continued to be used for its original purpose for 100 years. It was established as a co-operative effort at a time of hardship due to the exorbitant price of flour. A petition was presented to the Mayor and Aldermen on 24 September 1795 by John Mozeen, William Spencer, John Thornham, George Willey and Richard Pidd with an outline proposal for a new mill to be built by a group of subscribers, and 'humbly beseeching' their Worships' advice and assistance. As a result, £350 in donations augmented the subscriptions (one shilling and a penny per week for four weeks, and sixpence a week for four weeks more, i.e. a total of 6/4 or about 32p from each subscriber) to the extent that the mill, with five sails, costing £2,200 was built between 7 June 1796, when Sir Henry Etherington laid the foundation stone and gave a further £100 to the cost, and 7 June 1797 when the mill became functional. Various millers were associated with it as managers or workers, including Thomas Clark, 1803, William Smith, 1806-7, William Stephenson, 1810-15, Slater Eyre, Henry Tinegate, 1851, Richard Borwell, 1855, and Robert Pollard, 1871. At first there had been 1,435 subscribers but by 1847 there was such a demand for flour that a new share issue was promoted, increasing the number to 2,500. This made possible the building of a new steam mill costing £1,312. Later in the century, after some financial difficulties in the 1850s, new rules were formulated, permitting the sale of flour to the general public, not just to share-holders. Flour from the Anti-mill was sold at certain shops only. About 15 or 20 of these outlets existed in the first half of the last century, not only on or near Holderness Road but in the town centre also. The mill continued in a financially stable state until 1895 but closed in 1897. Richard Sizer, engineers, had the premises soon after the mill's closure; later John Harwick, wagonette proprietor, was at No. 218 and probably used the yard for his vehicles and stabling; by 1921 Fenton and Parrinder, builders, and J. W. Harrison, cabinet maker, were at the site, and a club used part of the

The Anti-Mill near Balfour Street, after the addition of a steam mill.
(*Courtesy of Humberside Leisure Services*)

15

premises in the mid-20s. Lorrimars, the corn factors, were there until after World War Two, when there was still a yard entrance — now filled with small shops.

7. **Waddingham's Mill** was in the middle of what is now the row of shops between Holland and Victor Streets, set back with a house and garden in front of it. It was worked from 1803 (the earliest date I can find) by John and later Nathaniel Waddingham, who introduced steam power in addition to the windmill by the mid-century. It was still called Waddingham's mill in 1875 when Joseph Rank rented it, although John E. Tinegate had been there before Rank. By this time it was, according to *The Master Millers*, the history of Rank milling, 'more a subject for an artist than a practical miller'. Someone did paint the mill, as the picture was used as the frontispiece of *The Master Millers*. The artist was Frederick Hunt Jarman, who had a grocer's shop in the early 1880s at 10 Argyle Terrace, Holderness Road, at the corner of Barnsley Street. Much later, when Jarman and Rank met and the latter was far beyond the status of a young man undertaking his first enterprise, Jarman offered the picture to Rank, who bought it for £25, a high price, set rather tongue-in-cheek, it would seem, by the artist himself. This anecdote was recorded in a letter sent by an old lady to the *Hull Daily Mail* in 1949 and cannot be corroborated, nor are the present whereabouts of the picture

Waddingham's mill, where Joseph Rank first set up in business. Dated 1875, the roadside trees are already planted, the hinterland (of Holland Street, etc.) is merely fields and the chimney of Hodge's mill is discernible at the left hand edge of the picture, which is a copy of a painting.

(Picture courtesy of Rank Hovis McDougall)

known to the archivist of Rank Hovis McDougall, although a line reproduction was used in centenary advertising of 1975 as 'The Founder's First Mill'. Frederick Hunt Jarman was obviously a relative of William Jarman, grocer, first of Church Street, Drypool, and then of Jarman and Flint, wholesale grocers, and mayor in 1904, as both Jarmans were born in Market Harborough. James Naylor was at the mill in its latter days, but it had ceased working by 1889 by which time the tower had gone. The rest of the premises had become the Victoria Hair Works, James William Shaw's curled hair factory, and the house in front was called Temple Cottage. This business continued into the early years of this century, but by then Temple Cottage had gone and the blocks of houses and shops on the main road had been built in front of the works.

8. **Bell's Oil Mill** was directly opposite the later Brunswick Chapel, within a slice of land surrounded by the huge tract owned by Henry Broadley. In 1831, Stickney, Bell and Petchell were merchants and seed crushers with an office at No. 1 Scale Lane and an oil mill on Holderness Road. In 1834 John Petchell of Wellington Place, Sculcoates, had a half share (a moiety) in this mill with William Henry Bell who lived and worked at it. By 1838 Bell was on his own as W. H. Bell & Co., merchants and seed crushers, the office still at No. 1 Scale Lane, mill and residence, Holderness Road. Bell was one of the members of the first reformed Corporation as councillor for Holderness Ward and was among the first group of councillors from that Corporation to be elected alderman on 1 January 1836. Despite the fact that he was declared bankrupt in April 1841 and thus resigned from the Council, the oil mill on Holderness Road apparently continued in Bell's name until Henry Hodge took it over in the 1850s. There was an auction of stock — casks, wedges, tools, weighing machines, *etc.*, but the amount and type of material did not seem sufficient to offset the bankruptcy; however, a dividend was offered to creditors a few weeks later. In 1851 Henry Hodge was living at No. 11, East Parade, had an office in High Street, an oil mill in William Street, Drypool (jointly with his brother, William, later alderman, and mayor in 1860), and in 1857 had a mill built near Blaydes Staithe. From about 1855 to the 1890s Hodge's firm, later trading as H. Hodge and Son, with his son H. S. Hodge and son-in-law Joseph Thomas Robson, was oil milling at Bell's mill. A new warehouse was built for the firm in 1864 at 3-4 High Street and altogether it was a prosperous concern. Hodge lived for many years at Ivy House at the corner of the lane leading to the mill, a track which became known as Hodge Avenue and, ultimately, Morrill Street. In the left background of the painting of Joseph Rank's first mill (which was only a short distance from Hodge's) there is a high building which could be a mill tower without sails and next to it a tall chimney. This, dated 1875, gives the idea that the oil mill was worked first by wind and then by steam, and indeed a chimney is shown on the map of 1889. Henry Hodge was a well-known local Non-conformist;

it was he who laid the cornerstone of the Holderness Road Primitive Methodist Chapel (Bright Street) on 1 December 1862, and his name was perpetuated in the Hodge Memorial Chapel, Williamson Street, of 1872. Seed crushing continued at the mill until the last decade of the century and the mill buildings are still marked on the 1900 reprint of the Ordnance Survey.

9. **Rank's Mill** or **Eyre's Mill.** I think that most people in my life-time have called the old mill near Southcoates Avenue by the more famous name, but, when the Rank family left it in the 1860s, Salter Eyre moved in and the name recorded for the latter part of last century and into this was Eyre's Mill. Certainly the cottages were Eyre's Cottages. John Rank came to this mill in 1851. Originally from Sproatley, he had moved to Hull in 1842, after putting the Sproatley mill on the market in March of that year. He came to an unspecified mill on Holderness Road which I think must have been on the other side of the road, near where Lake View now is. In 1846 he moved to a mill in Southcoates Lane most likely opposite the later convent and then, finally, to the mill which still remains near Southcoates Avenue on Holderness Road. Here his grandson, Joseph, was born on 28 March 1854. Tenure of the Southcoates Lane mill passed to Joseph's father, James Rank, about 1851 but at first James must have been working on his father's account there as it was not until 1853 that he set up in business on his own. According to *The Master Millers*, John Rank retired in 1857, having three years previously sold the Sproatley mill at which his son-in-law, Slater Eyre, had been for some time the miller. If this is so, he must have been unable to sell the Sproatley mill in the spring of 1842 when he advertised it in the *Eastern Counties Herald:*

'Sproatley in Holderness. To be sold by Auction by Mr. J. Jaram. At the Constable Arms in Sproatley on Saturday the 2nd day of April next at 2 o'clock in the afternoon. Subject to such conditions of sale as will be then and there produced.

All that capital Newly Erected BRICK WIND CORNMILL, containing two pairs of French stones, with Corn Screen, Cylinders and Dressing Machine all new and complete; and also all that good and substantial BRICK AND TILED MESSUAGE or DWELLING HOUSE with Stables, Cart Shed, Piggeries, Granary, and the Garden, Orchard and grass PADDOCK thereto adjoining containing altogether 3 ROODS or thereabouts.

The above property is very eligible for Investment, the Mill is situate in a good Circuit, in full Business, and capable of grinding upwards of 40 Quarters of Wheat per week; the Granary will hold 80 Quarters of Corn; the Garden and Orchard are well stocked with fruit trees in full bearing and with the Paddock is in a high state of cultivation. This Estate is Copyhold of the Manor of Burstwick, fine certain and small, and subject to a yearly rent to the Lord of 2½d. A considerable part of the purchase money may remain on security of the Premises, and immediate Possession will be given. Further particulars may be known on application to Mr. John Rank, the owner, at Sproatley or to Messrs. Iveson and Son, Hedon.'

During the winter and spring of 1841-2 other windmills were for sale in the area, Drypool, Cottingham, Roos, Beverley Road Sculcoates, North Newbald, Goodmanham (wind and watermills) and Waltham (Lincs.). Perhaps the Sproatley auction did not reach the price John Rank expected and so he put Slater Eyre in as miller until it was eventually sold. Then, for what must have been a few uneasy years, another of John's sons, William Rank, had charge of the Holderness Road mill before emigrating to Australia in the late 1850s. By 1861 the mill was in James Rank's name, but Slater Eyre was living there at the time of the 1861 census. In 1863 John Rank died; soon after this James moved to the Stepney mill and from then on, until the early years of this century, Slater Eyre was the miller, a tenure of over 40 years. Of all the windmills on Holderness Road it is the only one to have survived, the shell a landmark, the cottages used as dwellings, a fruit shop, a coal office and the premises of a monumental mason during different periods of this century. The ground floor of the mill has been used as a workshop and at one time for a cycle repair business. The complex has very recently become The Mill, the latest public house on Holderness Road.

10. **A Corn Windmill** was on the North side of Holderness Road in the 1850s between the present Ferens' Haven of Rest and Lake View. This mill remains a mystery because of the vagueness of the addresses in Somergangs and on Holderness Road, but it is clearly shown on the 1853 Ordnance Survey, with a ditch along the main road in front of it and a bridge to give access. The sequence of names in White's *Directory* of 1851 indicates that Henry Clark was at this mill before moving to Southcoates Lane by 1855. There were Clarks, millers, for many years in Marfleet Lane (Craven Street); Henry may have been one of this family. Again, if the order of the names as they appear in the Holderness Road entry can be trusted in Kelly's *Directory* for 1857, there is but one conclusion to be drawn: that James Rank was for a time in the late 1850s concerned with this mill, across the road from his father's. This makes me wonder if this was the mill to which John Rank first came from Sproatley. In 1871 a retired butcher, Joseph Kemp Firth was living in a presumably new house on the site, Crescent Villa, which remained until 1925, when Mr Spruit built three houses in its place, one of which is called Crescent Villa, perpetuating the former name.

11. **Sutton Ings Mill** was a corn windmill behind the farmhouse which faced Holderness Road next to the Four-in-Hand. The house remained until after the last war and was for many years from the 1920s occupied by the Haldenby's who had a pork butcher's shop at 153, Holderness Road, near Courtney Street. Mr Haldenby's grandson told me that there were millstones for thresholds at two doors at the back of the house, and a pile of

bricks in a corner of the garden showed there might have been a building, but there were no signs of the foundations of a tower, so it may have been a post mill. Harder evidence of the mill's existence is on the 1853 and 1889 Ordnance Surveys as Sutton Ings Mill is clearly marked in this position. Joseph Kellington was here in 1823, James Plews in 1840, and in 1851 Richard Baxter, who it seems was both miller and mine host of the Four Alls next door. Between 1872 and 1889 Charles Snell was the miller and latterly, in the 1890s, George Duke. The mill was not in use in 1897 and probably was demolished by that date.

The Holderness Road panorama included other mills, not on the road itself. There was the mill next to the Windmill Inn, worked by the Naylors and then the Tinegates for many years, and Jackman's flax-carding mill behind the Blockhouse mill was also worked by wind power. In Dansom Lane were at least three windmills visible from Holderness Road: Dale's mill, the tower of which remained so far into this century as to be remembered by many people alive today; the five-sail Subscription mill, built by similar financial means and for the same reason as the Anti-mill; and Turner's whitening mill further on down the lane. Behind the six-sailer was another corn windmill beyond Hume Street, almost on Dansom Lane, and in the present Craven Street were the Marfleet Lane mills of the Clark family. At the slight bend of Southcoates Lane as the road followed the course of an old stream and at its junction with the later New Bridge Road, was a mill in the position that Teanby's and later Fletcher's bakeries were situated, and there was another windmill on the north side of Southcoates Lane further down. Family information has now confirmed my theory that this was Rank's, as Teanbys were also milling in Southcoates Lane, and I think that must have been the mill that had occupied the bakery site.

Imagine coming into Hull along the Holderness Road in the early part of last century: a flat landscape, open to the sea winds, populated by these wind-driven giants, but with the black sulphurous smoke of more modern factories visible as one neared Dansom Lane. The smoke replaced the sails on the skyline as the century progressed; the demise of these windmills came as steam replaced wind as the motive power.

STATELY HOME

Holderness House was built on Summergangs Common after the enclosure. The first house, called Summergangs Hall, was bought by John Kirby Picard from Thomas Hall in 1785. Picard was the man whose name appears on the Hull Lead Works penny token of 1812, with a portrait, not of the man but of the works, and again on the halfpenny token, but this time with the Picard crest of a lion sejant and the motto *Esse quam videri* (Be, rather than seem). The white lead manufactory was on part of the Guildhall site.

Holderness House, or Summergangs Hall, as it appeared in the early 19th century.

Picard modernised Summergangs Hall about 1800; it had been a rather plain classical house but he gave it a fashionable Italianate appearance by the addition of rounded projections and iron balconies. He sold it to John Broadley in 1814, but as there are no entries for either Broadley or the house from 1814 to 1822, he evidently did not live there. In 1823 Dr John Ayre (chiefly remembered for his essay 'On the Pathology and Treatment of Cholera' in the *Lancet* of 28 April 1832) leased the house from Broadley as a retreat for female mental patients, on the lines of the Friends' Retreat near York. Dr John Alderson and Dr Richard Casson continued here after Ayre went to London in 1826; three years later James Alderson took his father's place and the Summergangs Retreat continued until 1836. The estate was sold by Broadley's executors to the Jalland brothers, Boswell Middleton and William Empson Jalland in 1838. They immediately replaced the old house with the present one in a neo-Elizabethan style that was ahead of the fashion of the time. Called variously Jalland Hall and Orange Hall, Holderness House became the stronghold of the Liberal party. James Clay, M.P., stayed here as guest of the Jallands and the house became the target of the wilder element of the Tory faction on a number of occasions. Jalland dealt with one such foray in decisive manner. Having heard that the Conservatives were on their way up Holderness Road, he sent a message to the Gas Works and alerted the police, so that the Holderness Road street lamps were put out and the police were ready to make a charge near Durham Street. On another occasion the Tories routed the Liberal band along the

21

road and the poor musicians took shelter in the thickly shrubberied grounds of the house until the Tories had dispersed, but left the instruments with their tell-tale orange ribbons under the bushes till morning.

B. M. Jalland himself was described in glowing terms by the *Hull Free Press:* 'The Adonis of Holderness House . . . His is the head of Apollo, but his ancles *[sic]* are those of Mercury . . . The young men are all envious of his good looks, and every year he grows younger on purpose to vex them . . .' and, more seriously, 'Holderness House is the fortress of the Orange party in Hull, and the name of its owner is a tower of strength. Our political Cupid has done the cause some service; year after year he has worked long and zealously for Reform. A Liberal he was when Liberalism was not fashionable among men of his means.' Jalland did not marry until he was 61 and then had a daughter and three sons between 1852 and 1861; Mrs. Jalland continued to live at Holderness House until her death in 1909.

In 1907 130 acres of the estate were bought by James Reckitt in order to build the Garden Village, but a considerable area of ground remained around the house and there was a field at the back. The house and grounds were next occupied by T. R. Ferens until his death in 1930 and since then, by his will, the house has been a retirement home for 'gentlewomen'. The term may be old-fashioned, but the house continues graciously as Ferens wished. The ashes of both Mr. and Mrs. Ferens are buried in the garden. Holderness House is now more visible from the road, as Dutch elm disease took many mature trees and dense undergrowth and saplings were removed when the diseased trees were felled. A new wing was added some years ago and there are plans for the extension of the home. The field at the back, which Mr. Ferens allowed to be used for Wesleyan, Temperance and other galas, was sold after the war and prefabs. built on it. These have since been replaced by the bungalows of Acacia Drive. The grounds of Holderness House form one of those green areas within the city, a haven for wild life. Foxes are frequently heard and seen in the district.

THE MID-NINETEENTH CENTURY

'A period of most wonderful transition' was the description of the mid-century by Prince Albert during preparations for the Great Exhibition of 1851 that was to demonstrate to the world the strength and diversity of British industry. Hull provided a display of its products and the imports which fed industry elsewhere. Not only had the area of Hull increased dramatically by the boundary changes of 1836, but since that time the population had also increased, a real increase, not due merely to the added population of newly-acquired land. By the middle of the century there had been considerable building on the south side of Holderness Road, but on the north side there were few dwellings at that time. As the development of the north side began with the building of Wilton Terrace in 1851 and the road began to be more fully populated, it is convenient to take 1851 as a time of transition of Holderness Road as it became an important town thoroughfare.

Up to 1851 domestic building had been largely confined to the south side. There were cottages and Cobb's Buildings from Albion Place (the top end of Naylor's Row near the Windmill Inn) to a site at the corner of Thomas Street where three Model Houses were being built that year. Flanking South Parade (Williamson Street) on the main road were two rows or terraces of houses that had been there since before 1823: nearer the town ten houses called Somerstown and on the other side 11 bigger houses called East Parade. Somerstown remains with some modifications, but substantially as it was, except of course, that the houses have long ago become shops. The English Presbyterian Church of 1875, the pointed roof of which can be seen above the Green Man nowadays, cut into East Parade, and later development near Field Street took more of it. East Parade was the address of people in a fairly good situation in life: Rev. Thomas Morton, Mr. John Nornabell, David Cobb, Mail Coach proprietor, and Henry Hodge, seed crusher, before he moved out to Ivy House near Bell's Oil Mill.

Prospect Place (not to be confused with a street of the same name near Drypool Church) had four houses in 1851, the start of the later Field Street, so called because Mr. William Field, tea dealer, grocer and seedsman, lived on the corner; his address, the same house, became Field House, 12 East Parade, in 1861. There were a few houses then up to Kerman's Square, a terrace at right angles to the road, with fair-sized back gardens on the town side of the houses (approximately in the position of the Salvation Army hall). Two houses only (one of which was Stockton House, home of Francis Reckitt) stood between here and the Holderness Steam Mill, just before the railway, which was laid in 1852-3 to carry goods to and from the new Victoria Dock of 1850.

After the railway were a few houses (Robert's Terrace) up to the Nag's Head Inn, with Nag's Head Lane (Waller Street) beside it. Even in 1851 there were small courts and terraces here: Mary's Place, John William's Place, Cooper's Place and Blenkin's Place. Who the other names referred to I do not know, but in Nag's Head Lane itself lived Elizabeth Blenkin described as 'Independent' and head of a household consisting of her son-in-law, Joseph Taylor, a butcher, his wife and son, William Blenkin Taylor. It may have been that Elizabeth's independence was due to owning the terrace which bore her name. Cottage Row, seven houses close to the main road (the shops which were demolished in recent years to widen the road at the Mount Pleasant junction) were immediately after Nag's Head Lane, and set back were the grey-brick villas of Hornsea Parade, where lived in 1851 Thomas Petchell, miller, among others.

That was early 19th-century 'ribbon development' on Holderness Road as far as Marfleet Lane (Craven Street) — four rows of houses, Somerstown,

The 3-storey building at the corner of Wilton Street dates from the 1850s. This view is from the early years of this century.

For comparision, the same view in 1973. Some of the more distant buildings have now been demolished.

East Parade, Cottage Row and Hornsea Parade, with a few houses in between.

The north side of the main road presented a different picture. At the top of Dansom Lane, a few houses called Lawford Street turned the corner gracefully with the rounded building that is there today. These have been in use since 1850 or before. The end one, with the Holderness Road sign on it, was No. 1, even though there were Nos. 1 and 2 at the other side of the road. There was then a gap which is still there, and the area bounded by the main road, Wilton Street and Dansom Lane, was just starting to be used for house building. This prime plot of land belonged to George Wilkinson, architect and surveyor, town councillor and look-alike for Sir Walter Scott. Before that the land had belonged to John Graham (or Graham-Clarke) of Newcastle, maternal grandfather of Elizabeth Barrett Browning, acquired as a bequest, with other properties, from Thomas Mowld of Sutton. No. 1, Wilton Terrace was already up and occupied by Mr Thomas Eeles, monumental mason, who used the space beside the house as his stone-yard. Six houses were under construction in Wilton Terrace in 1851, but in the next year or two there would be a row of 12 family houses occupied by professionals and tradespeople.

Marshall's Mill with a smithy beside it and another in front was directly opposite East Parade and there were in 1851 four houses nearby occupied by Robert Laverack, blacksmith, William Marshall, George Priestley, corn miller, and Richard Field, commercial traveller. Then, until Bartle Mill was reached, was open ground, possibly fields, except for a corn or seed kiln and Poplar Cottage where Thomas D. Ball, the master of the British School in Dansom Lane, lived with his wife, two nephews and his niece, Anne Akass, a pupil teacher. Around Bartle Mill were several small dwellings. In one of them lived and worked Heneage Hodgson, of Withernwick, boot and shoemaker, 23-years-old, his Liverpudlian wife, his daughter and his grandmother. Beeton Street, with Hume Street across the bottom, was already cut through, one of the earliest side streets.

At the other side of the projected Victoria Dock line was the six-sail windmill, also with buildings and dwellings around it, and behind, near what became Courtney Street, Rose Cottage, the home of John Graves Clark, bottle merchant. A rope works was already established hereabouts and by the late 1880s had a considerable area of Burleigh Street, with rope walks below the high level railway.

This was suburbia! Further on were the mills described earlier; a cowkeeper; Durham Street ready for new houses to be built; Holderness House surrounded by trees, and Southcoates Lane opposite; two cowkeepers down Jalland's Lane (Laburnum Avenue); then Leonard West, grocer and tea dealer in Silver Street, but with a brick and tile works down in the fields behind his house, Summergangs Cottage; and then the cluster

Nos. 31 and 33 Holderness Road, dignified 'town houses' of the mid-19th century.

of two farms, other buildings and the inn which made up the area called Mile House, before more open countryside. Two more windmills; a brickworks at the present Willows, the claypits now forming part of the park lake and the fishing pond at the back of the Willows: with the toll-keeper's house at Ings Road corner, that was Holderness Road in 1851.

Beyond the town boundary at Ings Road were the old farmsteads that remained into the 1930s and after: at the corner of Ings Road (Crooked Billet site); the corner of the present Marfleet Lane opposite St Michael's and another behind the present church grounds in Marfleet Lane; Leyfield House in Four Alls Lane behind the inn (Four-in-Hand) and the mill house and mill fronting the main road. Rose Cottage or Salt Ings Farm (it had both names at various times) was before the drain bridge, one of the windows of the house bricked up to avoid window tax, as I was told as a child. The position of the drive into this farm is still marked by a fine horse-chestnut tree on Holderness Road, one of a few that used to be there. Across the drain, still on the north side of the road, was another of these brick and pantile farmhouses, and at the Saltshouse Lane junction, the 17th-century Eastfield House and cottage which are still there: Eastfield House, much altered, has been there since 1680; Saltshouse Cottage, beside it, since about 1600. Armitage House farm, with Bilton Drain beside it, was just at the point where the drain crossed under the road. This was Bilton Brig or

Eastfield House, much altered in its long existence, derives from a building on the site, dated 1680. It is now the premises of John Parkin & Son, Funeral Directors.

Bridge, the limit of the ancient King's Highway, but, in 1851, three miles out on the turnpike road to Hedon.

CHAPELS AND CHURCHES

As milling dominated the industry of Holderness Road, so Liberal Non-conformity dominated attitudes; thus, 'Chapels' come before 'Churches' in this title. In an age when newly enfranchised men voted as their employers voted and with neighbourhood examples of public men of strong character and principles, people's opinions on a wide variety of daily issues tended to be similar, whatever favour the person wore on polling day or wherever he worshipped. Even so, there were strong class divisions, not least between the Wesleyans and the Primitives, differences levelled only by the Second World War. I noted with amusement that, although Henry Hodge and his son were prominent at the Primitive Bright Street Chapel, nevertheless Henry laid one of Brunswick's foundation stones about 13 years later. There was still a distinction between the Wesley (opposite Ellesmere Avenue) and Portobello up to and after the Second World War despite the apparent fusion of different aspects of Methodism at a higher level.

Some marriages are said to be made in Heaven but on Holderness Road in the latter part of last century and the beginning of this a fair proportion of local marriages were made at one or other of the local chapels, as they were strong in social activities, none more so than Brunswick. In some respects the Chapels' influence as 'community centres' was greater than the schools' but the compulsory basic education offered by the State secular system gave opportunity for greater choice of leisure and social activities.

Kingston Chapel. Although in Witham, this large Wesleyan chapel was very much a part of the life of Holderness Road, attracting large congregations from a wide area. It was designed by J. Simpson in the Greek Revival style, the facade having four Ionic columns supporting the pediment. Worshippers passed through the iron gates into a wide flagged forecourt with a weeping ash in the centre and up a flight of steps to the entrance. The chapel could accommodate 1,600 people and on many occasions did so. It cost £8,000 to build, was opened on 14 June 1841 by

Kingston Chapel, seen here about 90 years ago, was opposite the Windmill Inn on Witham. The house on the extreme right became the Midland Bank, was bombed and rebuilt and the building now houses a branch of Mencap.

Robert Newton, President of Conference, and continued as a major centre of worship for a century, succumbing to the bombing of 1941. People have told me of the feeling which existed between this Wesleyan congregation and the Primitives who worshipped at Bright Street chapel not so far away. Cabs stood at the rank outside the Kingston Chapel at the turn of the century, but whether or not the generally better-off Wesleyans would ever employ them on a Sunday is an interesting point to ponder.

Holderness Road Chapel, otherwise known as Bright Street. The foundation stone of this large, impressive Primitive Methodist Chapel was laid on 1 December 1862 by Henry Hodge, seed crusher. Members of the Hodge family were well-known supporters of Primitive Methodism in Hull and at the stone-laying substantial sums of money were given by Henry Hodge himself, also by his brother, Alderman G. Hodge, Henry's son, William, and son-in-law, J. T. Robson. Closer to the road than Kingston Chapel, it nevertheless had its flight of steps leading to a pilastered entrance. Inside, it was circular in form with a gallery right round, the front of which was enamelled white and gold. Add to this a large central gasolier of fifty lights hanging from a flower boss and a picture is formed of some splendour. Jane Garbutt, reminiscing about the chapel in 1886, recalled that the Mothers' Meeting attracted more than 100 women every Monday afternoon and that there was no lack of helpers when in 1876 tracts were distributed through The Groves, Holderness Road, Williamson Street, Drypool and Hedon Road just after an even larger Primitive Methodist Chapel, the Hodge Memorial, had been registered in Williamson Street. Bright Street Chapel was yet another victim of 1941 bombing.

St. Andrew's Church. St. Peter's, the parish church of Drypool, was near the Old Harbour and for centuries had served the hamlet situated on the east bank of the river. The parish boundary, however, included that wide area of Southcoates which became populated as Holderness Road developed, and so, by the mid-19th century, St. Peter's was no longer in the centre of its parish population. In 1856 a mission hall had been opened near the top end of Beeton Street and services were held there until the new church, St. Andrew's, was consecrated on 20 July 1878. Later that year, St. Andrew's became the parish church of Drypool with St. Peter's as a chapel of ease. The new church was a plain brick structure with some stone decoration, build on land given by the Liddell family. It was intended that the church should have a tower and spire when funds permitted, but this never happened. The geometrical 'west' window faced the road and the access door was at the west end of the north aisle, giving on to Abbey Street. At first the church path curved on to Holderness Road, for Abbey Street started at Williamson Street and was not cut through to the main road until the beginning of this century.

Drypool Vicarage was Stockton House, tenanted by Francis Reckitt for some years before the church bought it for £820 in 1862 during the incumbency of Rev. Charles Campe. In 1893 this vicarage was sold and a branch of the Hull Savings Bank built in its place. A new vicarage at the corner of Lee Street, designed by F. S. Brodrick, was erected that year and was in use until 1923. The Beeton Street mission hall had been used for various activities, but in 1909 the Abbey Street Rooms and later, 1923, the Church Hall, were added next to the church and the mission hall sold in 1921. Abbey Street Hall is remembered by many East Hull people, women especially, for very popular tea-dances were held at the end of, and just after, the war when life was otherwise more dismal than had been expected. A youth club also flourished there until the 1970s. Change and re-development of the area led to such a decrease in population that the church was demolished in the early part of 1984. A Housemartin Housing Association hostel for young homeless people has occupied the Holderness Road end of the site since December 1987, with Housemartin flats for the homeless round the corner in Abbey Street.

St. Andrew's was more often called Abbey Street Church than by its proper title; possibly many people thought Abbey had some religious significance here. However, the street was named after Ald. Thomas Abbey, a man cruelly likened to a turtle by the *Hull Free Press*. At the end of the last century Ald. Mayfield wrote of Ald. Abbey: '... there was no better-known public man in Hull than Ald. Abbey (who afterwards bought the cow that gave milk to the babby)'. What the last phrase refers to, I do not know; the bootseller alderman must have had qualities undetected by the *Hull Free Press*.

Brunswick Chapel. On 11 June 1874 an 'iron school-chapel' was opened by the Wesleyans in Durham Street on land purchased the previous year. The activities organised there, in which Mr. Ferens was an active participant, drew young people to the Sunday School in crowds, and full congregations for the other services, so that it soon became clear the place was too small. The foundation stones of a new chapel were laid on 4 November 1875, and in less than three years Brunswick had become one of the great spiritual and social centres of Holderness Road. The chapel was not as large as Kingston or Bright Street, but internally gave the impression of size because of the light from the windows under the rounded arches of the facade and on each side of the body of the hall. In 1884 a large house and garden in Durham Street were bought, the garden upon which to build a Sunday School, the house as the minister's residence. Henry Hodge had been a stone-layer at the building of the chapel; his widow laid one of the stones of the Sunday School on 28 May 1886. After the opening of East Park the following year and up to 1939, it was usual to take a walk along the tree-lined Holderness Road to the park after service in the summer or after Sunday School. This stretch of road was by some people called The Promenade because of this practice. Great care was taken with the planning of all the buildings connected with Brunswick; they were modern to the extent of being described as pioneers of school planning. In 1903 further changes took place and the Brunswick Institute offered a range of activities for all ages, including sport, for the seven acres on Holderness High Road opposite Ellesmere Avenue, had football and cricket pitches, tennis courts and a bowling green. Brunswick was such a focus of life of the area that in 1914 the chapel seating was increased by 100 places and five more schoolrooms were added. The present chapel replaced the old one in 1962; the houses of Sperrin Close and Charnock Avenue were built on the Recreation Ground about 1980.

St. Columba's Church. As with many places of worship a temporary structure served here until a permanent church was built. From 1914 to 1929 the temporary church in Laburnum Avenue was used. The brick church on the corner is the second on roughly the same site: the ground plans of the 1920s church and the post-war rebuild further back overlap. The foundation stone of the first permanent church here was laid on 7 October 1926 by the Princess Royal, George VI's sister, the Princess Mary. The ceremony was not performed at the church but at the Cecil cinema where a thanksgiving service was being held and purses received towards the Hull Church Extension Appeal. During the service the Princess pressed a button by which the foundation stone of St. Columba's was laid, the church being consecrated in January 1929 by Archbishop William Temple. The building was never completed, although enough had been constructed for the life of the church to go on. In one of the last raids of the war, and a nasty one at that, the night of 13/14 July 1943, St. Columba's was destroyed by bombs. Building the second church did not begin till the late 1950s. Its

Brunswick Chapel near Durham Street.

position was sufficiently different from that of the first church to warrant a re-dedication and this time the Princess Royal came in person to the site, with a procession headed by the Police Band and accompanied by the Lord Mayor, Ald. L. Science, and the Sheriff, Mr. Eric W. Mackman. This was on 4 October 1958; the building was completed in 1960. The original 1914 St. Columba's still serves as the Church Hall. Throughout I have referred to this church as St. Columba's as this is the common East Hull way, rather than saying 'the church of St. Columba'. Perhaps this seems a pedantic point to mention, but not so when the church's dedication is changed in print (as I have seen sometimes) from the dove-like name of the saint to that of the discoverer of America!

East Hull Presbyterian Church built in East Parade in 1874-5, was a high Gothic building of red and greyish brick with a large traceried west window facing Holderness Road. It was bombed, but not demolished, in 1941 and services continued in a schoolroom until after the war. The church which is its closest descendant on Holderness Road is the **United Reformed Church** opposite Westcott Street, housed in the back of two houses, numbered 442-4 in 1939, the front part of the building altered after bomb damage. The present church is small, a far cry from the 1,000-seater church of 1874, but a comfortable and dignified setting for the services has been made from adjoining back rooms of the houses.

East Park Baptist. The summer of 1913 may have been the end of an era nationally, but Holderness Road beyond the Crown Inn witnessed the construction of many new houses and the regimental Drill Hall, the opening of the park extension and boating lake and the dedication of two new churches. The day before the ceremony in the park, on Sunday, 7 June 1913, the main foundation stone of the East Park Baptist Church at the corner of Southcoates Avenue was laid on behalf of the Yorkshire Association of Baptist Churches by the President, Mr. S. Sharp of Morley, and eight other commemorative stones were laid by friends of the church. The hall, still there next to the church, had been used for worship since 1909 The church itself is of red brick with stone tracery to the west window in the unobtrusively charming facade. It has accommodation for a congregation of 400 people.

Portobello Methodist Chapel started its existence in a wooden mission hall in the early years of this century. The permanent chapel was opened by the Primitives in 1906, designed in a quite distinctive style by Gelder and Kitchen. The building cost £4,500. The stone-laying ceremony was extensive and the stones, originally set in the lower courses of the wall and retained when the chapel was pulled down in 1984, were again reset in a low wall near Portobello Street. The chapel entrance was on Holderness Road and the building, of red brick and stone, had two curious tower-like structures at the front which, I believe, housed internal stairways. There was a balcony on three sides of the main hall, the front woodwork of which was taken to Cave Castle in 1984. The new chapel on the mission site meets today's needs in that the main hall has a stage and blackout and is used both for services and other meetings. There are also rooms for small classes or devotion and the means whereby lunch can be provided for the Monday Leisure Day. This has become a great attraction; the members are mostly women of the retired generation, but the range of talks and activities is quite wide and the social impact incalculable. Mrs. Jane Garbutt wrote of the regular attendance of 100 women to the Bright Street meetings on Monday afternoons; Mrs. Joan Bruce can expect a regular Monday morning attendance of more than 100 men and women at the Leisure Day.

Kingston Wesley. This chapel was built in 1913 outside the city boundary when houses were already built up on Holderness Road beyond Marfleet Lane, on the north side of the road up to the drain bridge, Ellesmere was started and Shaftesbury being built. There was as yet no Maybury Road. That came in 1925, roughly the same time as Lake View, Lake Drive, the Parade between them and Waldegrave Avenue. Smaller than the Portobello Chapel, the Wesley can nevertheless hold 550 people on the ground floor and in the U-shaped balcony. There are small classrooms off the sides of the chapel, and at the back the quite spacious schoolrooms have been altered slightly since the war and a large porch added. At first it was just 'the Wesley Chapel on Holderness Road', but after the last war, when the remains of Kingston on Witham were demolished and some items from there were brought to the Wesley, Kingston's name, too, was added, a name which will therefore be celebrating 150 years of attachment to Methodism in East Hull next year (1991).

St. Michael and All Angel's, Sutton Ings. A plain brick church is at the corner of Marfleet Lane on a site given by Mr. F. A. Scott, with a church hall beside it. On 6 May 1913 the *Hull Daily Mail* commented that the area around the then new church was 'more than a village now. Where a year or two ago were green country lanes and fields there are now streets laid out in big estates. Within a stone's throw, too, is the Ferens' Recreation Field and the locality is dominated by the huge Wesley Chapel which will shortly be opened.' St. Michael's was part of the Archbishop of York's Church Extension Scheme and (this again from the *Hull Daily Mail*, 23 April 1913): 'The builders are a Glasgow firm and it is constructed in a way rather differently from buildings in Hull.' This refers to the present church hall, the original Church, and it was painted in 'a delicate harmony of pink and cream ... a pleasing contrast to the green country field'. The opening service on the evening of Monday, 5 May 1913, was taken by the Bishop of Hull (Dr. Kempthorne: the next day came the announcement that he was to be Bishop of Lichfield), and the following Sunday (Whit Sunday) by Canon Joseph Malet Lambert, the Rural Dean. After the First World War the brick church was built and consecrated in 1927. It is a very plain structure with no outside decoration, neither transepts nor tower and equally plain inside. The present bell, I believe, was bought as a result of collections in the church and neighbourhood as a thanksgiving for peace in 1945. The vicarage was at first on St. James' Parade, then The Gables, No. 996 Holderness Road, but in the mid-Thirties a large vicarage was built behind the church in Marfleet Lane.

LATE NINETEENTH-CENTURY DEVELOPMENT

When in 1856 Thomas Walton described 'A day on the Holderness Railway', he took the train from the Victoria Dock Station, which was the inner terminus for the Withernsea line. He tells us that the village of Sutton with its white church tower surrounded by old and rugged trees, is visible to the north. As the century progressed, this glimpse would not be afforded to the traveller because of buildings extending outwards from Holderness Road in the side streets. The town's industry was increasing, especially along the River Hull, greater import/export activity was possible with the opening of Victoria Dock, and the number of workers required, especially unskilled labour, led to a spate of house-building to provide homes near enough to the places of work. Holderness Road became, not a road of factories, engineering works and timber yards as Hedon Road was, but largely a residential area for families whose breadwinners walked to Hedon Road, Drypool and Stoneferry.

The first houses on the road had been occupied by families of men in a good way of business, profession or trade. Somerstown, *etc.* were the suburbs of their time. However, a person walking to them from the town through Witham or Church Street (the latter named, on Capt. Phillip's map of 1720, the King's Road to the Common), would have his nostrils assailed by the smells from the muck garths which lay between Witham and Church Street at the bottom of Coelus and Hyperion Streets. On their 'many acres of land garnished with balmy hills and dales', as H. J. Whiting of the *Hull Free Press* ironically described them, night soil and other detritus accumulated and manure merchants had their livelihood. A correspondent to the *Hull News* was more forthright in his description: they were, he wrote, 'Alpine ranges of lively rottenness, decomposing, fermenting, steaming upwards in blueish reek, oozing downward in black putrescence, and dissolving in the hollows into unctuous, inky foul smelling rivers, which crawl laggingly among the spongy soil, and dye its glutinous slime a deeper black.' The rancid smells from mills crushing seeds to make linseed oil and cattle cake would be wholesome by comparison.

The sanitary reforms of the mid-century and after eventually rid the town of this evil, and — a slow process — public awareness of the importance of a sufficient supply of pure water for proper domestic hygiene and sanitation was brought about by the various Public Health Acts, the first of which became effective in 1851.

Fronting the muck garths on Witham was a series of courts or alleys, Chafer's Alley, Clean Alley, *etc.*, similar to many in the old town: small enclosed areas approached by tunnels through the buildings facing the street. In the old town at the time of the visits of Edwin Chadwick's team of Sanitary Commissioners in the 1840s many of these alleys were described in the official reports, the tunnels penetrating buildings of three or more storeys and opening to tiny courts, 20 feet square, perhaps, and, if fortunate, with a pump for communal use. Admittedly the Commissioners said that the flags in some of these courts were scrubbed as clean as the deck of a ship, but the lack of ventilation, sanitation and pure water were sources and perpetuators of all manner of diseases, of which cholera was the worst.

How much better, then, to live in the almost rural situation of one of the terraces in Nag's Head Lane, even though these, too, were built before important bye-laws came into force to improve the standard of housing. True, there was a fellmonger's yard at the bottom of the lane, and a ketmonger's place rarely smelt of roses, but here also were fields adjoining the inn, used for grazing and where a horse doctor had his premises, and open country within minutes' walking distance beyond Marfleet Lane (Craven Street). The terraces off Nag's Head Lane were the first to be built in the side streets off Holderness Road. I imagine they would be brick and pantile like many a row of cottages in Holderness villages, but have no way of knowing if they were of one or two storeys. John William's Place, for example, was a row of five houses, each about 11-feet wide. There was an open space in front, but the small back yards were enclosed because of a long building at the back of the row. Water from the Stoneferry Waterworks was available from a communal tap in each terrace and gratings are marked on a mid-1850s map, possibly indicating their linkage to the then new East District drainage system.

Holderness Road's side streets were built in a rather haphazard way, not a regular progression from the town. **Durham Street** was the first of the long streets to be opened up and even now it is easy to see that the different houses and terraces of this street were built over a long period of time, even excluding the developments of the 1980s. Durham Street originated in a Victorian episode of self-help through what could be termed a building society or a housing association. An initial meeting was held in February, 1850, at which Mr. James Beeton outlined the working of a Freehold Land Society. An East Hull advocate and supporter of such a venture was Leonard West of Summergangs Cottage, but it must be remembered that he had had a brick and tile works hard by, even though by now it was in the hands of another member of the family, Robert West, so that, however laudable the scheme, Leonard may have had an eye to business. The result of just one meeting was the formation of the Hull and East Riding Freehold Land Society, the aim being to secure a vote for members as freeholders. About a hundred shares were signed for before the meeting closed. During the next few weeks, more public meetings were held, including one that attracted an attendance of six or seven hundred working men to hear James Taylor give an account of a similar scheme in Birmingham.

Durham Street was not recorded in the census of 1851, for, although the street had been constructed to its present length by 1852 at the latest, it was not until some time after that there were houses and occupants. In 1861 the census showed 33 heads of households, including six women. Places of birth of these people and their spouses showed a great similarity to the pattern of population of Holderness Road itself, where about a third of the householders and their wives were born in Hull, a third in villages of the East Riding, mostly Holderness, the final third originating from more distance parts of the country. So it was in Durham Street in 1861: of 57 known places of birth, 18 were Hull, 20 the East Riding, and 19 beyond. Most of the children of these couples, however, were born in Hull: from a total of 59 children only 12 were born outside the town, showing that the breadwinner was settled in Hull, for the time being at least.

Ten years on, the census returns show that people were still coming into Hull to find work and by then there were 69 households in Durham Street, including the new terraces, Carlton Terrace, William's Grove, Richmond Terrace, Providence Place and James' Place. Of 125 places of birth recorded for the householders and their wives in 1871, 40 were Hull, 30 the East Riding, but 55 of these people were born in places as far apart as northern France, Devon, Hereford, Greenock, Tewkesbury and, as before, there was a fair sprinkling from Lincolnshire and East Anglia, especially men in the milling and ancillary trades. The average age of the head of the households in Durham Street dropped from over 46 in 1861 to 39 years in 1871, and of 139 children in the street in 1871, 106 had been born in Hull.

It was to be expected that the population in the early days of a self-help scheme would be generally of mature enough years to be established and able to continue the payments for the house. With no national pension or Social Security provision, and a completely different attitude towards money from that of today, to enter into a contract to pay only coppers per week was a great undertaking. With one exception, a dock labourer, the people of Durham Street in 1861 were tradespeople or had a regular income, from a Trinity House pension, from house rents or from their work as millers, coopers, bricklayers, clerks, policeman or farmer. They were not rich people, but neither were they of the poorest class. Of interest are two mariners' widows, Elizabeth Ansdell and Hannah Salmon, both recipients of Trinity House pensions. Hannah, widow of William Salmon, received 18s. (90p) per week from December 1856 to January 1862 when she died, aged 65. Mrs Ansdell, however, was much younger and had seven children, five of them under the age of 14 when she first received a charitable pension from Trinity House in 1859. At that time the two oldest sons, in their mid-teens, were working, one a clerk and the other a pupil teacher at 'the marine school', presumably Trinity House. Her pension was 6s. per week (30p) but she supplemented it by taking in boarders. In 1861 her boarders were James Stuart, master boiler and oil refiner, his wife and son, the James Stuart of the statue near Garden Village.

The influx of workers from elsewhere continued to be shown in the 1881 census and, as far as the residents of Durham Street were concerned there were more coming to Hull from distant parts of the country than from the nearer villages of the East Riding. Some families had moved about a lot: for example, Robert Wilson, a 42-year-old labourer from Thirsk had five children born in various places — Normanton, Huddersfield, Leeds and Harrogate. There were still the migrants from Lincolnshire, but in this street in 1881 there was a greater diversity of occupations among them, for, as well as men working at the mills, there were also Lincolnshire-born engineering and ship-building labourers, clerks, a police constable and a coal dealer. There is much more a suggestion that people came to Hull to seek work, rather than bringing a trade to a place where it could be exercised.

Chestnut Villas. At one time Alfred Gelder lived at No. 1, and Joseph Rank at No. 4, but the best remembered occupant must be Dr. E. M. Townend at No. 3.

Woodlands, now occupied by a branch of Dr. Barnardo's.

Durham Street was built early and for a long period formed a kind of boundary, as the character of Holderness Road changed about here. Probably this is fixed in my mind because for long enough Durham Street was a stage on the tram and trolley-bus services. Nevertheless, opposite Durham Street was a double-fronted villa, Durham House, which was a private residence from the 1850s onwards and, as a tuberculosis dispensary from the 1920s, was beside the lane to Morrill Street clinic until well after the Second World War. Next to Durham Street was the creeper-covered Durham Villa with a pillared entrance and battlemented walls concealing a small side garden: this is now Bush, Optician. These, with Ivy House opposite Brunswick Chapel, were three early detached residences of some size which were followed in the 1860s to '80s by single houses and small groups of gentlemen's residences clinging around the edge of the Jalland estate at Holderness House. Woodlands is the best surviving example, but behind the facade of Pramland next door at No. 346 is Saxby House, T. R. Ferens' home before he moved into Wilton House and then to Holderness House itself. The block of four near Jalland Street was Chestnut Villas and in the last few years of last century Alfred Gelder was at No. 1 at the street corner, Joseph Rank at No. 4 and, with Ferens across the road, there was a trio of Hull worthies!

Between the 1880s and the end of the century, dignified and in some cases unusual, houses were built from Southcoates Lane towards Mile House. Of these, near Westcott Street, was Westcott House where Thomas Priestman lived; next door, now the Wood Grange Residential Home, was the turretted house of Frederick I. Reckitt, and at the corner of Lee Street as it became, on land belonging to the heirs of John Lee, Esq., was Drypool Vicarage, designed by F. S. Brodrick and built in 1893 at a cost of £1,725. That is now the Pink Panther Home. The three houses now between Lee Street and Summergangs Road were products of the early years of this century. They look all of a piece to the casual observer, but are in fact three distinct houses built at different times. Burnbrae and The Cedars were already occupied by 1908, but St Mungo's at the corner of Summergangs Road replaced Summergangs Farm several years later when the road was cut through the farm land. By the 1920s, when the Reckitts and the Priestmans had moved elsewhere, Westcott House belonged to Dr. Eddie, Burnbrae to Dr. Wildeboer and St Mungo's to Dr. Divine, three of East Hull's best-known doctors — and Dr. Ethel Maude Townend was in Alfred Gelder's former house near Jalland Street. But we move too quickly!

Because of the comparatively late start to domestic building on Holderness Road, the worst evils of overcrowding and bad conditions for the working people were avoided. From the 1850s, when Wilton Terrace was built, there had followed on the main road, blocks or terraces of family houses, with little front gardens and often with attics. The blocks near

The East Hull Silver Band poses at the rear of Saxby House. The gable of No. 1 Chestnut Villas is seen top left at this turn-of-the-century picture.

Wood Grange, home of Francis I. Reckitt, sold in 1913 for £1,420. In the 1930s and after World War 2 used by the Christian Scientists, and now the Wood Grange Residential Home.

(*Architect's drawing, courtesy of Mr. G. Hempshall*)

Courtney and Brazil Streets, now shops, and Poplar Buildings between the overhead bridge and Nornabell Street are different in that they are of three storeys and were most likely tenements from the start. These are the only three-storey buildings of this kind on Holderness Road, but similar examples can be seen on other main roads of the city. Poplar Buildings retain some terra-cotta decoration typical of the 1880s; the only other row with a quite distinct style and decoration is Lorne Terrace up to the corner of Buckingham Street, the block where Pharaoh's Video shop occupies premises that were once Boot's the Chemist's. The round-headed, grouped upper windows are reminiscent of Wilton Terrace, but what plant form inspired the decoration at the ends of the curves. Cocoa-pods?

For the most part these terraces of family houses pre-date the nearby side streets. Those near Holland Street, however, had a slightly different history because there was a succession of buildings here, including, briefly around 1910, the East Hull Roller Skating Pavilion and, in the mid-20s, tennis courts on the site used by Woolworth's in the 1930s. The 1901-2 Bethesda Chapel was behind in Holland Street until it was bombed, and since then, until this year, there has been an open space where the foundations of the chapel could be traced among the weeds.

Holland Street was relatively late, but once started, the terraces off it were built almost simultaneously with the front houses so that by 1900 the following terraces were both built and occupied: Gladstone and Salisbury Villas, Wilton Avenue, Albert Villas, Mable's [sic] Villas, Ernest Avenue, Eastern Villas all on the south side, and Ellen's, Beaconsfield and Churchill Villas and Crossland Avenue on the north. Who were Mabel (or Mable!), Ernest and Ellen to be in such distinguished company?

Most of the long straight streets of Holderness Road of both the last century and this, i.e. from Courtney to Portobello, were pretty well all of a piece, put up in one spate of building, often by one builder and almost saved from dreadful monotony by the use of red and yellow bricks, slight differences in decoration, 'rents' (spaces) between blocks of houses and by the terraces intersecting the older streets. The old rectilinear field patterns also gave a uniformity. For example, the 1889 map of Courtney Street is more like a regular mosaic than a jigsaw. Only at the ends of streets, where old streams and drainage ditches wandered in anything but straight lines, does a rectilinear arrangement cease. At the end of Durham Street a ditch which joined the Lambwath Stream cut across at an angle, leaving the end plots triangular or kite-shaped. At the bottom of Kent Street where Bright Street cut across at an angle (and I believe it followed the line of an old ditch or stream), Edwin's Terrace and Eugenie Terrace were tucked into an awkward plot of land and had tunnel entrances to their back alleyways.

Of course, the streets between Dansom Lane and the railway were in general earlier than Courtney Street and beyond, but Kent and Studley Streets at first were much shorter than they ultimately became, not because of the rate of house-building, but because the streets themselves were not constructed in the early days, unlike Durham Street which was its present length as a roadway before any houses were built.

Sometimes the names of the terraces, like those mentioned in Holland Street, give a clue to their date, just as the Boer War names of Steynburg, Middleburg, *etc*. Streets on New Bridge Road are indicative of their time. Popular or merely well-known names in politics or among royalty and gentry were used: Albert Place and Victoria Terrace in Beeton Street, the latter of early build, 1850s, as it was a row of 16 houses (or two lots of eight end-to-end) with two communal back yards reached by two tunnels; in Courtney Street a Gladstone Terrace 30-odd years earlier than Holland Street's Gladstone Villas (but then, the Old Man had a long political career); and Wesley Terrace in Courtney Street. There were also the picturesque names like Willow Grove in Durham Street, Floral Grove and Oaklands Avenue in Arundel(1) Street and Myrtle Grove in Nornabell Street (but Myrtle could have been just another girl's name, like Rhoda, next to it).

Some names are to be found close at hand. The ill-fated Ellis's Terrace, which opened directly from the main road between Bright and Studley Streets, may well have been erected by John Ellis, builder, who in 1876 was living at No. 66 Holderness Road, just four houses away from the new terrace entrance. Mawer's Terrace, tucked in behind Station Parade (from the railway crossing, Pedder's tripe shop to Lipton's on the corner of Courtney Street in 1939) and of which the sycamore tree near Mount Pleasant is now the only trace, took its name from being near Charles Mawer's grocer's shop in the 1860s and '70s. Westcott Street must have got its name from the Wests' Summergangs Cottage, which was somewhere behind the present parade of shops on land long held by the West family. The house was there, occupied by Alfred West, into this century.

The level crossing, which bedevilled traffic for more than 100 years, came with the Victoria Dock Branch Line, a rapidly built length of railway, opened for freight on 16 May 1853, less than a year after powers had been obtained for its construction. Southcoates Station, designed by William Botterill, was already marked on the 1853 Ordnance Survey. A major upheaval of the latter part of the last century was the building of the overhead railway, an ambitious project intended to ring the town without the problems of level crossings. It was a far-sighted scheme, operative over a century after its 1885 inception. The overhead bridge, however, now proves a bottle-neck, and the effective width of Holderness Road, whatever else has been relieved elsewhere, is constrained by the width of the bridge. It has also for many years been another of those 'dividing lines' on the road, its character changing radically from that section between the level crossing and the bridge and seeming narrower than it actually was because the shops had no forecourts. Beyond, between Nornabell and Durham Streets, the

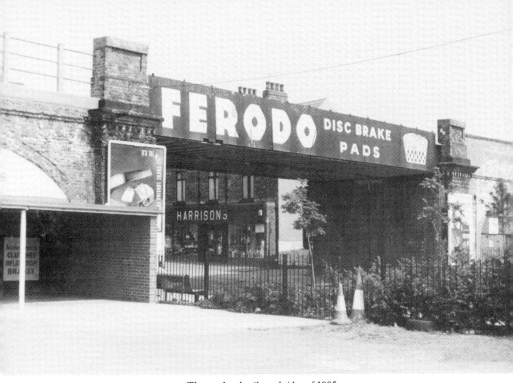

The overhead railway bridge of 1885.

Jesmond Gardens. Now used as warehousing, these were the premises of the Hull Tramway Co. in the days of horse-drawn trams.

rows of family houses had had front gardens and so the shops have forecourts; in much more recent times this has allowed space for bus stops off the main traffic lanes.

When there was only horse-drawn traffic and not so much of that, there were coach services along the road to various places. An advertisement in the *Eastern Counties Herald* for 10 June 1841 gives a glimpse of one such service:

'The public are respectfully informed that the HULL and HORNSEA COACH will commence running for the Season on Monday next, 14th inst., from the ROYAL HOTEL and LONDON TAVERN every afternoon, Quarter to Five; and PROCTER'S OFFICE, Land of Green Ginger, and CHAFFER'S, Silver St. FIVE O'CLOCK instead of Four as formerly, thereby allowing Passengers coming by the West Mail Train, sufficient time for Refreshment and giving Hull Merchants an opportunity of receiving their West letters; and will return from HORNSEA each morning at EIGHT until further Notice. Performed by R. J. Chaffer, A. & R. Procter, Proprietors, who beg to return sincere thanks for past favours and trust their future Exertions will ensure a continuance.' Service!

By 1861 there were Carmen's Buildings in front of the present Jesmond Gardens. As the Hull Street Tramway Company's service from Savile Street to Lee Street did not start until April 1875, I think that there must have been some coach or cab service along the road before the horse-drawn trams. The present Jesmond Gardens warehouse of Brookes' Hardware was the depot and stables of the Hull Street Tramway Co. which also had some premises, stabling *etc.*, opposite the Crown Inn. A single track of 4ft 8½ins gauge was provided with passing loops, and the trams, in reddish brown livery, each pulled by two horses, continued the service until 4 June 1899, at which time there must have been considerable disruption while electrification proceeded to enable the City of Hull Tramways service to open on 10 April 1900.

However, people who moved to this area in the latter half of last century were prepared to walk to work, to friends' houses and to the country. Mr. Ferens was well known because he walked to and from work at Reckitt's and there are still memories among older people about pleasant encounters with him. One old lady told me recently that as a small girl she and her sister went regularly to a music lesson, and, on seeing them with their music cases, Mr Ferens would exclaim, 'Ah, the two young ladies and their music!' Another old lady told me that on her 21st birthday, in her best clothes, she went to have her photograph taken (she didn't say so, but I expect she went to Harry Abba at No. 48 Holderness Road, in the old Somerstown) and on her way home met Mr. Ferens, who recognised her as one of the Reckitt's workforce and complimented her on her appearance. These may seem trivial anecdotes in themselves, but to have been remembered for 70-odd years shows the importance of meeting with this well-known man and how his character and popularity became influential in East Hull. These were acts of neighbourliness to fellow-residents of the same road, incidents which perhaps were more highly rated by some than his great munificence to the city.

Nevertheless the better-off kept carriages. There is a carriage arch in East Parade still remaining, another near Jesmond Gardens, also one at Carlton House and here and there in the side streets, although some of these may have been for horse and cart transport used in small businesses rather than for a family conveyance.

Largely residential, Holderness Road from Dansom Lane to the park gates would be fairly recognisable if we could go back in time. There was work, however, not only in the shops and in domestic service of the bigger houses, but also at the remaining mills, in the rope works of Burleigh Street and behind the Anti-mill, at the Hope Iron Works, at the joinery works of Beecroft and Wightman in Burleigh Street, at several brickworks situated in the fields behind the main road houses and, of course, in the building trade itself. Here were jobs apart from the waterfront, the railways and the expanding firm of Reckitt's. Not all was plain sailing, however, especially

Carriage arch a few doors down Dansom Lane, most likely for a small business when constructed with the houses in the early 1850s. *(Photo: 1968)*

in the mid-1880s when many men, including skilled workers, were unemployed after the completion of Alexandra Dock. It is too simple to say that the end of the dock project was the only cause, but it was estimated that there were more than 1,000 unemployed men in East Hull and poverty to the extent that soup kitchens were opened in Williamson Street Chapel schoolroom. The East Park project gave work to many, as the park was laid out at a time just after the dock construction ended and opened in 1887.

Victorian philanthropy towards the Holderness Road area extended well into this century because of Mr. Ferens' gift of land to enlarge East Park and his provision of the almshouses, the Haven of Rest. The Reckitt family also, by building the Garden Village for its workers, provided a pleasantly tree'd area to be enjoyed by others. However, true Victorian philanthropy-with-a-purpose came to Holderness Road much earlier, in the form of the James Reckitt Public Library of 1889. The powers of the 1850 and 1855 Public Library Acts had not been taken up by Hull Corporation, despite attempts in 1857, 1872 (following the establishment of state-funded elementary schools) and again in the early 1880s. On 21 September 1888 James Reckitt called an influential meeting at which he offered to prove his belief that a Free Library could be run on a penny (1d) rate by subscribing an annual sum equal to such a rate on all the rateable property in East Hull (about £500 p.a.!) and also £5,000 for the building and initial books, to be repaid in the same way as for free libraries that had been set up under the Acts.

The library thus provided was opened on 10 December 1889 on part of Kerman's Square. A new reference library, the gift of Francis Reckitt, was added the following November. East Hull Library opened at a time when the first generation of Board School children were approaching adulthood and when the first children of compulsory education were about nine years old. Both circumstances, I believe, in an era of self-help were the cause of the library's great success, for the majority of people could not afford to buy newspapers, let alone books. This pioneering effort led to the adoption of the Libraries Acts' provisions in Hull, and therefore the James Reckitt Library was the first of the free public libraries in the town.

Next door to it is a later addition, the East Hull Baths, built on Kerman's Square in 1897. Not the first of their kind (for baths had been provided by the Corporation at the Stoneferry Waterworks in 1845 and also in Trippett near North Bridge in 1850), these baths were near dense housing and, being on a tram route, were accessible to many people. They provided for personal bathing at a time when the 'bathroom' was a zinc or wooden tub in the kitchen (if that), as well as for recreational swimming safer and cleaner than in the Foredyke Stream. The red granite foundation stone is so unobtrusive now as to be missed, but it records the occasion on 10 June 1897 when it was laid by the mayor, Henry Morrill, J.P., with the names of other officials present.

By the end of the last century with all the streets from Dansom Lane to Buckingham Street and from Naylor's Row to Morrill Street, Jalland, Lee, Aberdeen and Portobello Streets built, some wholly, others in part, the city was stretching out in this north-easterly direction and the road was assuming its present form. Many of today's shops were still houses with front gardens, trees planted to line the road in the 1870s were maturing, and the section of East Park from a track which became Summergangs Road to a point beyond the park-keeper's lodge was a pleasant place for Sunday afternoon walks. Holderness Road by 1900 was modern in the sense that it had long had the amenities of street lighting, drainage to keep it from winter flooding, pavements and a tramway service, but the road of these days was only half the length of the present thoroughfare which now extends to Ganstead Lane. There was not, as yet, much development beyond Mile House, Ings Road was still the boundary and beyond that were open fields and farms, hedgerows, trees and ditches — the countryside.

THE SCHOOLS

The first residents of Holderness Road were obviously go-ahead people wanting the best for their children. A major piece of evidence for this comes in the contrast between the Newcastle Commission's average figure for the proportion of children in weekday schools of all kinds during their survey of 1858-61 and the situation on Holderness Road. The Commission's overall result was 12.99% of the country's children. From the census returns of Holderness Road itself, admittedly a small sample, a different picture emerges:

1851: of 210 children up to and including 14 yrs. 35% were 'scholars'
1861: of 187 children up to and including 14 yrs. 51% were 'scholars'
1871: of 298 children up to and including 14 yrs. 51% were 'scholars'

This is before there were State-funded schools in East Hull and parents had to rely on the National (Church of England) School in Drypool, the British (Nonconformist) School in Dansom Lane, St. Mary's Roman Catholic School in Wilton Street and small private establishments like Raynard's Academy in the house Richard Field had left near Marshall's mill, or Miss Caroline Walker's Ladies' School in Wilton Terrace. Here and there also were small 'schools', some of which would teach the three Rs sufficiently well for the expectancy of the times. After State intervention in education by the Forster Act of 1870, committees called School Boards were set up, the chairman of Hull's first Board being Sir Henry Cooper and its secretary John O'Donoghue, who lived at No. 2 East Parade in the 1870s. The Board Schools formed after the 1870 Act, beginning in this area with Courtney Street, rapidly became like village schools with tight loyalties and overt rivalries. A century later, when Hull's first comprehensive school, David Lister, opened, one of the staff's first tasks was to create new relationships between children from 'Bucky' and 'Chappy' and elsewhere, because the rivalries had been built up even before their grandparents' days.

Just inside Dansom Lane, the building of the 1838 **Holderness Ward British School** still stands, a product of the British and Foreign Schools Society and supported in its time by local Nonconformists, including the Reckitt family. It was staffed by a schoolmaster and mistress; during the 1840s the lady teacher was Miss Pitman, sister of Isaac, the inventor of the Pitman system of shorthand. This school closed in 1872, once the Hull School Board was established after the 1870 Act, as it was expected that the projected **Williamson Street** school, built in 1875 for 750 children, would more than compensate for its closure. However, the pressure for Board School places was so great in the 1880s that the British School premises were used temporarily during the years 1881-5. The building, of two storeys, was used in the 1950s as a furniture repository and workshop by the firm of T. T. Cass and Sons, cabinet makers at 2, Wilton Terrace since the 1880s and now, much changed, the school is occupied by A. L. Barnes, Ltd., Joiners and Building Contractors.

St. Mary's Roman Catholic School, where the children were taught by the Sisters of Mercy, was opened in 1856 in Wilton Street. The school continued under the Sisters' care until 1954 and then, until 1972, by the Local Education Authority, after which it was demolished.

Courtney Street School was the second of Hull's Board Schools. It was built in two storeys directly on to the street with no area or railings between the school wall and the footpath except in the recessed centre section which was embellished with stone coursing, the three crowns of Hull and the inscription 'Board School'. There were gables at each end of the building, distinguished with barge boards and a gable over the central rectangular upper window which had an area of fancy yellow brickwork above it. The school was opened in 1874 to accommodate 250 girls, 250 boys and 250 mixed infants, but the general population of the district increased so rapidly and the school population increased also after attendance became compulsory in 1880, that, in the early 1890s, Courtney Street, along with many other Hull Board Schools, was extended by the addition of a junior department. Williamson Street's extension was opened in 1894, Courtney's a year later.

Buckingham Street was a slightly later Board School and is the oldest State school in the city still serving its original purpose. Its outward view is a lively red-brick building with a cupola, little gables and embellishments of terra-cotta sunflowers and a neat reminder of its date, 1882. Had the resolution of Evan Fraser been accepted at the Hull School Board meeting of 1 November 1882, this school would have been named after Thomas Stratten, but other practicalities prevailed and that name was used by the school in Londesborough Street instead. Buckingham Street school's original accommodation was soon too small for the growing population of the district and so this school, too, had an additional department built, at the other side of the street, in 1894. The school's role has changed over the years according to population needs and educational policies and is now, since 1988, Buckingham Primary School for five to eleven-year-olds, the building across the road being used as a Youth and Community Centre.

Hornsea House School was a private school in a grey brick house on the left side of Hornsea Parade, as approached from the main road. It was a school for young ladies run by Mrs. Mary Rowell wife of Charles Rowell of the same address. This was listed in White's *Directory* for 1895; in 1901 it was in the name of Miss Brown who must have been a teacher there, as the Rowells continued with the school into the 1920s.

Studley House opposite St. Columba's housed a ladies' school from the 1880s to the 1920s at least. The first mention of it is in Kelly's *Directory* for 1889 under the care of the Misses Augusta and Ada Walker. About ten years later it had passed into the hands of the Misses Keer who continued there until well after the First World War. A range of subjects was taught; discipline, as remembered by an old lady I knew, was firm, and the overall impression was of a 'good' education of the older type.

Archbishop William Temple, at the bottom of Westcott Street, was officially described as a Voluntary Aided Church of England School. It was the replacement or descendant of a much older foundation, St. Peter's Church of England School which functioned in Church Street, Drypool, from 1829 to 1864, when a new school building, incorporating stone from the Citadel, was opened in Prospect Place, Drypool. It is not irrelevant to mention this school, as children from the Wilton Street, Thomas Street area attended it in the 1920s. Prospect Place was bombed in 1941 and the school discontinued; its modern successor, again not on Holderness Road itself, but catering for children of the area, opened in 1954. Since the 1988 reorganisation of Hull schools, Archbishop William Temple School has come wholly under the Humberside Education Committee, no longer Voluntary Aided, and is now called Westcott Primary School.

Alderman Cogan's, another school tucked away off the main road, in Whitworth Street, Southcoates Avenue, was also partly under the aegis of the Church of England as a Special Agreement (C.E.) school. Its history goes back to the mid-18th century when Ald. William Cogan endowed a school in Salthouse Lane for the education of poor girls. From 1889 to 1950 it had premises in Park Street. The inscribed stone from above the original Salthouse Lane doorway was taken from one building to another and the last time I saw it was in the Whitworth Street school hall where it had been painted as part of the wall. As well as the founder's initials and the date 1755, the stone contains the initial letters of the following inscription:

O Most Transcendent Being,
Aid And Sanctify This Gift,
O Lord Jesus Christ,
That Many Orphans May Say
Amen.

Alderman Cogan's School in Whitworth Street was for some years a secondary modern, then a middle school (5-13) and since 1988 has been a Voluntary Aided Primary School for children between the ages of five and eleven.

The Willows, another small private school, continued up to the Second World War in the house called The Willows opposite Portobello Street. It catered for both boys and girls and was run by Mrs. Betty Hall, who I think was generally called, without disrespect, Madam Hall. The children wore brown and yellow uniforms.

Portobello Hut. In the early 1930s a two-teacher school existed in the wooden mission hall which pre-dated the Portobello Methodist Church. The hut stood on the same site as the present chapel and contained a long room for two classes and another room where there were billiard tables and a sink. Outside were some old lavatories which I, as a 5-6 year old regarded as places to be avoided! The space between the hut and the chapel was a playground of rough black cinders. Many children starting school there passed through the very capable hands of Mrs. A. M. Wilson, a small neat lady, a widow I believe, who lived in Eglinton Avenue. The school was used at a time when the city boundary had altered (1929) and the Local Education Authority was in the process, under the directorship of R. C. Moore, of making changes to Hull's education system by the addition of new schools built with the recommendations of the Hadow Report (1926) in mind. **Flinton Grove** was the 'flagship' school of this re-organisation and in East Hull it was followed by **Maybury,** to which Infants' Department I went as soon as it opened in 1934, with Miss Campbell as Head Mistress. The mixed Senior School opened the following year and the lower junior classes were accommodated there until the whole school building was completed. We moved into the Junior Department, the most westerly of the long range of buildings, in 1937, with Miss G. Needham as the first Head Mistress.

During the late 1880s there was national anxiety that Britain was falling behind other countries, notably Germany, and that if educational standards were not raised there would not be enough skilled workers in the chemical and engineering industries. This has a familiar ring. In Hull, to meet the needs of some older children, on a selective basis, three Higher Grade Schools were established to provide an education with greater scientific emphasis than was possible in the Board Schools. One such Higher Grade School opened in 1893 in **Craven Street,** but the complex of buildings also housed infant and junior departments for neighbourhood children. Craven Street was a fee-paying school and pupils came from country districts as well as Hull. So popular was it that in its latter years it was very crowded and a new school was needed.

In 1926, the new school in James Reckitt Avenue was opened and named after Canon Joseph Malet Lambert, Vicar of Newland, 1881-1912, Rural Dean, and a tireless worker in the cause of education in Hull. He had been

Chairman of the School Board and continued actively on various committees, especially concerning secondary and higher education, and was the first Chairman of the Council of Hull University College at its inception in 1927. **Malet Lambert High School** became a Secondary Grammar School after the 1944 Education Act, a 13-18 Comprehensive with Hull's reorganisation following the 1964 Act, and since 1988 caters for pupils aged 11 to 16. Craven Street School itself continued to cater for children of all ages in its area; some time after the Malet Lambert opening a senior school was formed as a follow-on to the infant and junior schools already there. This became Craven High following the 1944 Act, but was closed when the David Lister Comprehensive School opened.

Thanet Infants' School with accommodation for 240 pupils opened in 1955 when the outer reaches of Bilton Grange Estate were being built. It was followed by a slightly larger Junior School two years later. It occupies an extensive site along Holderness High Road in the locality formerly called Armitage Field and now the two schools accommodate children aged five to eleven as **Thanet Primary School.**

No list of schools would be complete without mention of the Sunday schools attached to the various chapels. In 1856, the same year as the building of St. Mary's Roman Catholic school in Wilton Street, a building that served as both school and chapel, a mission room was opened in Beeton Street as an outpost of St. Peter's, Drypool. Here, in 1861, a Sunday School was started by the Church of England which pre-dated the building of St. Andrew's Church by 17 years. This was also before the Nonconformist chapels and Sunday schools on Holderness Road, the Methodists in those days being served by Kingston Chapel on Witham. There were Methodist day schools in the town, but the major development of Holderness Road came at a time when proposals for a State system of education were being discussed in many quarters. This fact, perhaps, and the money needed, were limiting factors to the establishment of further Nonconformist day schools. However, the Chapels, as soon as they were built, Brunswick in particular, introduced vigorous programmes of activities for all age groups that must be classed as educational, and their value, especially in the period to the last war, must not be under-estimated.

For specific private tuition there have been a number of music teachers, including Mr. and Mrs. Pocock who advertised in 1910:

'**High School of Music,** 33, Holderness Road. Mr. Edward Pocock (tenor), Signor E. Baraldi's pupil (London), Professor of Singing and Voice Production. The Resonator in Singing thoroughly explained. Mrs. Pocock, from the Royal Conservatoire, Leipzig, Professor of Violin and Pianoforte.'

Many East Hull women will remember also:

'Miss Alice Pickles, M.R.A.D., R.L.L.S., A.S.A., Teacher of Dancing, 25, Telford Street.'

INTO THE TWENTIETH CENTURY

The small terrace houses in the side streets were usually four-roomed 'sham fours' that had a front door leading straight into a living room, a kitchen at the back, and often the stairs twisting up from the kitchen, boxed in like a cupboard. In the very poorest sham fours the bedrooms would be partly in the roof space, so that the ceilings were oddly shaped. Gradual improvements in minimum standards provided better accommodation, some with small entrances at the bottom of the stairs leading up from the front, not the back of the house, bay-windowed parlours and tiny sculleries jutting out into the yard. However, because of the limited area which could be allotted to the ground plan of each dwelling in a terrace, the vast majority were pretty basic. Back-to-back houses were unknown in the vicinity of Holderness Road as far as I am aware; by these I mean two terraces built on either side of a common wall, so that each row of houses had only front doors and the occupants had 'neighbours' on three sides. Holderness Road terraces had back yards, the earliest ones without back access to them, but, following certain bye-laws, provided with a back alley and a yard door.

The appearance of long streets like Severn, Lee, Brindley and so on, about the turn of the century, tells us that there was a market for larger, better-quality housing in East Hull than had previously been available on such a large scale. Houses in these streets were built for people who walked, cycled and used public transport, houses that had three bedrooms and in some instances shut-off back rooms with a passage leading from front door to kitchen. Attics were not common in the side streets but there are a few houses with them in Westcott Street. There was a certain cachet in moving further out along the road. To have started life in Barnsley Street and come to live in Brindley Street, say, was to move up in the social scale.

The older, more crowded streets near the railway and within smelling distance of One Long Pong (East Hull's name for Cleveland Street, matching the curiously named Wincolmlee at the other side of the river), although far removed from the squalid Old Town courts of the 1830s and '40s, were nevertheless well behind the times in possible physical amenities, let alone the general desirability of their situation — except that they were near to the cheaper shops, to work and to the town. In 1885, an advertisement for new Courtney Street houses had listed their good points:

'To Let, 5-roomed houses ... close to Southcoates Station, now ready for tenants; bay windows, gardens and coppers. More convenient and complete provision for comfort and health than any similar houses. Nothing in Hull at all like them.'

This was advertising on the band wagon at a time when the recently formed Hull and District Sanitary Association was pressing for better conditions, and no doubt a move into a new Courtney Street house from, say, Victoria Terrace in Beeton Street would have been a distinct

Lawford Terrace, Dansom Lane, with the lines between the houses, ready for washing day. Picture: 1968)

improvement. After 1893, when new bye-laws encouraged better practice in house-building, with regulations regarding dimensions of the little terraces, the provision of front gardens and bigger back yards, there were few such terraces built on Holderness Road anyway. The old streets and terraces were already built up, a mixture of rented and owner-occupied property, the family houses on the main road steadily being converted to shops, and the next available building land was still further out beyond Mile House. Jesmond Gardens was built into a strip that remained near the old Carmen's Buildings before the First World War, and an area of market gardening land at the back of Southcoates Lane to Mile House was built up by Joseph Ward, William Atkinson and others to form Newcomen Street in 1910-ish as the start of chiefly 1920s housing, linking to the 'Engineers and Physicists' streets — Brindley and Telford were first with only a few houses in 1910.

One of the largest developments was not directly on Holderness Road, but behind Holderness House. The Garden Village, for Reckitt's workers originally, laid out and constructed on the old Jalland estate between 1907 and the First World War, contained, by the middle of 1913, 490 houses

With Holderness House grounds at one side and Wilton House on the other, a man takes a ride by pony and trap, while the little boy plays marbles in the gutter. A picture of about 90 years ago.

Family houses in Westcott Street, looking towards the main road. On the left, a pile of builder's materials shows that others are being built.

already with tenants and a further 66 still being built. It was designed by a local architect and expert in garden suburbs, Percy Runton, head of the firm of Runton and Barry who was also responsible for the layout of East Park Lake and for the Ferens' Haven of Rest, 1911. The rents of these extremely well-built houses varied according to style and size from 4s 8d (about 24p) a week upwards in 1913. The lower rented houses had varied amenities, such as coppers, pantries or wash-houses, but at the other end of the scale there were three-bedroomed houses with bathrooms at 7s (35p) or more a week. The majority of the houses had good secondary access at the back, now lined with garages at the ends of gardens, but in 1913 there were, of course, so few cars that the intention in providing the back roads was that the householders could get carts to the garden 'for manurial and other purposes'.

Popular ways into East Park were Westminster and East Park Avenues where there were small cafés and ice-cream shops; these avenues were made up of more of the three-bedroomed houses already described and built in the first decade of the century. Argyle Parade (also of the 1901-1910 period) from Allen's Pet Shop to the Willows, Aberdeen and Portobello Streets (before 1900) and other houses to Ings Road and beyond, gave cause for an extended tramway service. The tram shed with its lively facade of all kinds of embellishments, including the lions looking down from the top, in a rich terra-cotta that changed colour subtly according to the time of day and the season, made a terminus at Aberdeen Street from 27 March 1903, replacing the old Hull Street Tramway Co.'s depot opposite the Crown Inn.

The first residents of Aberdeen and Portobello Streets would have to go up the road for their shopping, and their nearest places of worship were Brunswick and St. Andrew's, Abbey Street, until the wooden mission hall was built for the Primitives near Portobello Street. Between the two streets was a row of nine large houses called St. James' Parade. Their front gates were well out of line with the rest of Holderness Road and caused it to narrow so much that there was little space between the nearest tram track and the kerb, a situation which in Leeds would have been called a Tram Pinch. It is curious that the first house in Portobello Street is called Waddingham Mount and the terrace across the main road, Argyle Parade, just as Waddingham's mill had Argyle Terrace near Barnsley Street across the road from it. I can offer no explanation for this coincidence.

By the time of the First World War, many of the long rows from Mile House to the mill and from the Southcoates Lane shops to the tram sheds had been built, Aberdeen and Portobello Streets with St. James' Parade in between, Portobello Chapel (1906) and its earlier mission hut and then nothing before East-thorpe just beyond the boundary. On the other side: a field between Westminster Avenue and Crescent Villa, more fields to Argyle Parade, Tower Grange and some other houses to Ings Road, with a ditch along the roadside and little bridges for house access. Beyond the

Holderness High Road beyond Marfleet Lane in the early years of this century. New semi-detached family houses face the old Four Alls public house.

(Picture courtesy of Mrs. E. Veal)

boundary, many of the houses on Holderness Road's south side up to Saltshouse were built before World War One and also the Wesley Chapel and St. Michael's Hall. Shaftesbury and Ellesmere Avenues were started about 1912 with some houses on the main road about the same date. Beyond the shops near Ellesmere (which were pre-1914 houses), the larger dwellings opposite Charnock Avenue open space are from the 1920s. Beyond these, except for the Four-in-Hand and the old farms was pasture-land, very little changed, I imagine, since the enclosure.

LEISURE AND PLEASURE

Not for nothing was East Hull and Holderness Road in particular dubbed the Christian side of the city. Until World War Two the places of worship greatly outnumbered the public houses, and of the latter three were inns of ancient origin, stopping places for travellers on the difficult journey across Summergangs Common. Coming in from Coniston, Sproatley and Preston villages, the first inn on the turnpike was the Four Alls, now the Four-in-Hand, as the **Ganstead** (now called the Swiss Cottage) was a product of post-war development after Longhill Estate was built. Neither is the **Apollo** an 'olde hostelrie'. The old pictures of Hull in the bars and lounges of the Apollo may be modern reproductions, but many of the other features are those of a late Victorian middle-class residence: solid cornices, ceiling bosses, bannister rails *etc.* The house was formerly Craiglands, at first in a considerable estate, but which by the 1930s had dwindled to the area now taken up by the car park. The coach house, now a separate residence, was also in the grounds.

The **Four-in-Hand** was at one time a double-fronted house with a high brown wooden hoarding all round above the eaves, with Worthington's Ales writ large in off-white lettering. The first written mention of this inn that I can find is in *White's Directory* for 1840, but it is highly likely that some kind of alehouse existed here on the turnpike before that. The name, Four Alls, persisted long after it was officially changed in 1890, even on turn of the century maps, and the oral tradition of 'Four Alls' was still there up to the last war, the name being used by some older people. Four Alls derives from a piece of doggerel which in one form runs:

A king I rule all; A priest I pray for all;
A soldier I fight for all; John Bull I pay for all.

In the doubtful *Johnson MSS* it is given as:

Ye king governeth alle; Ye parson prayeth ffor alle;
Ye soldyer fighteth ffor alle; Ye grave gettith us alle.

However spurious the latter version may be, the rhyme has a basis in some political situation of the 18th century which unfortunately I have not been able to trace. I used to wonder if the name was a variant of Four Ale Bar *i.e.*

The old Four Alls which became the Four-in-Hand. Picture of about 1907.

(Picture courtesy of Mr. A. Shaw)

where ale was sold at 4d a quart, but this may be due to my teetotal upbringing in which any small pub could be described in this derogatory way. In 1937 the new Four-in-Hand was built in the then fashionable mock Tudor style and with a red neon sign and externally it remains pretty much as it was at that time.

The **Crooked Billet** was built in 1967 on the site of Fussey's farm, Sutton Ings, a typical red brick and pantiled Holderness farmhouse set well back, with cowhouses and a yard at the back approached from Ings Road. Once this farm had been just beyond the Holderness Toll Bar, outside the town boundary of 1836.

The Mill has come into existence in the past year, through a sympathetic conversion of Eyre's Cottages. The mill tower remains, refurbished to some extent and used for storage, but the faded reminder of Wilcox's stout at 2s 6d (12½p — but how much stout would it buy?) has been obliterated from its sides. A capped tower, even without sails, would enhance the scene and make even more striking what has long been one of Holderness Road's landmarks. I wonder what Joseph Rank would have said of his birthplace being converted to a public house?

The second old establishment on the turnpike was the **Crown Inn,** of which mention has been made in connection with its other name of Mile House. There was an inn here in the middle of the 18th century at the time of the enclosure of Summergangs Common. It was a cottagey type of place in the 1930s and here again, as with the Four-in-Hand, a complete rebuild before the war resulted in the present building, not of mock Tudor, but more like 'cinema architecture' of the Thirties, matching the Astoria and the Woolworth's building of roughly the same date.

At the corner of Garbutt Street (Barnsley Street) in 1876 was Massam's, a beer retail shop which soon became the **Elephant and Castle.** So, although more than a century old, this is not one of the original turnpike inns, but was created when Holderness Road was becoming built up and populated. Across the road from the new houses and terraces for working people were open fields still, and the two nearer mills, the Anti-mill and Waddingham's. Even so, the terraces of Nornabell and Barnsley Streets were rapidly being built and providing customers for the Elephant and Castle. A long-serving respected landlord was E. E. Graves who, after 20-odd years as landlord here, retired to live at Arthurton House, nearly opposite Waldegrave Avenue, in 1910. He died in late March 1927, aged 76 and the *Daily Mail* carried an obituary, a somewhat unusual honour for a publican in those days. The Elephant and Castle has been extended from the original beer shop and taken in more of Albion Parade, the row of seven houses, now shops, that were built in the 1870s.

The widening of the section of road beyond the overhead bridge caused the demolition in 1988 of the **Nag's Head,** another old inn, another of those which had started life as a cottage alehouse, probably thatched, and had

The Nag's Head at the corner of Waller Street as it was in 1972.

been updated to the standards of later times. Being in a thickly populated area it was rebuilt much earlier than the Crown or the Four-in-Hand, in the cheerful style of the turn of the century, with mock pediments and other features of no structural significance. Its landlady for many years during the 19th century was Margaret Chapman who, some years later, after retiring from the Nag's Head, was described as a 'proprietor of houses' and so seems to have done quite well out of the victualling trade.

To offset the removal of the Nag's Head at the road-widening, the last remaining house of Hornsea Parade, Hornsea Villa, about 140 years old, was converted into the **Craven Park** public house. Hornsea Parade houses were set back with 60-foot front gardens when first built, whereas Cottage Row, originally seven houses from Waller Street corner, were flush to the pavement. Later development extended Cottage Row to the entrance of Hornsea Parade, leaving the larger houses behind. They were good family houses and the Craven Park retains sufficient features after its conversion for one to be able to imagine it as a dwelling of some comfort and style.

Soon after the Victoria Dock branch line was constructed in 1852-3 not only did it carry goods to Victoria Station on the new dock, but a passenger service from Railway Street was opened too as a convenience for the people of Hull. Southcoates Station was built to a design by William Botterill. Titus Waddington, of Leeds, was the station-master in 1861, but the suburban passenger service survived only until November 1854, even though its inner terminus had been changed to Paragon. Ten years later, when Paragon had become the terminus for the Withernsea line which ran part way along the Victoria Dock Branch, Southcoates Station was popular with East Hull people using the line. A beer retailer opened a shop at the corner of Beeton Street and by the 1880s the **Southcoates Railway Inn** was flourishing. It continued in business until bombed out of existence in the 1940s.

One of the ironies of Holderness Road is the 1980s conversion of the English Presbyterian Church into the **Green Man** near Williamson Street. The upper part of the 1870s church building is above the pub door and is thus not in the centre of the total frontage. I presume that neighbouring buildings, which may have been schoolrooms of the Presbyterian Church, were used in the conversion.

As though to compensate for the sparseness of hostelries on Holderness Road itself during last century, Witham was more than well-provided. Though not on Holderness Road now, the **Holderness Hotel**, another mock Tudor update, at the corner of Dansom Lane, was on the original turnpike and its original address was Holderness Road. It was there in the 1840s and perhaps earlier … but the changing fortunes, names and situations of Witham pubs would be a story on its own. The **Windmill Hotel**, however, is so much part of the total Holderness Road scene as to be included here, especially as it was another of the oldest inns along the road, having been known as a cottage alehouse since 1820 and the cottage itself before that. It was next to the mill run by the Tinegates in 1814, but this may well have been the mill 'near Witham' which gave the name of Naylor's Row long before Clarence Street was cut through. In the early years of this century the Windmill Inn was in the hands of William Wheatley, a brewer, of Mytongate. When Clarence Street was constructed in 1902, Wheatley had the old inn pulled down and the present one built with all its splendid tile work, including the windmills over the doors. People may have scoffed at the time and called it Wheatley's Folly but it is good to see that the little windmills and the rest of a handsome building survived the bombing of two wars and some of the more ruthless 'development' of the Fifties and Sixties. It thus remains as an interesting sight in an otherwise drab neighbourhood and a reminder of the original fortunes of the district.

Whereas the public houses have survived and multiplied, the cinemas of Holderness Road are now mere memories to an older generation, pleasant memories too of times before a television set was in almost every house and when a long evening of comfortable entertainment could be had for sixpence or a shilling. Friendships were formed in the queues as the showings changed twice weekly and some people went to more than one cinema in order to see more than two programmes in a week. There was normally a main picture and a lesser one, the 'B' picture, a newsreel, shorts in the form of cartoons and general interest, advertisements and in some places an organ was played for a sing-song. The interest in old films on television today springs from a generation for whom cinema-going was almost as much a part of life as going to school or to the shops.

The **Dreadnaught** in Naylor's Row was the oldest in the Holderness Road area. It opened in 1910 in the old Salvation Army Barracks, after the Army's new Franklin Street hall had come into use in 1908. The Dreadnaught accepted jam jars instead of admission money, I have been told, and it continued as a cinema for about ten years.

One of the Blitz casualties was the **Ritz** at the corner of Brazil Street. It

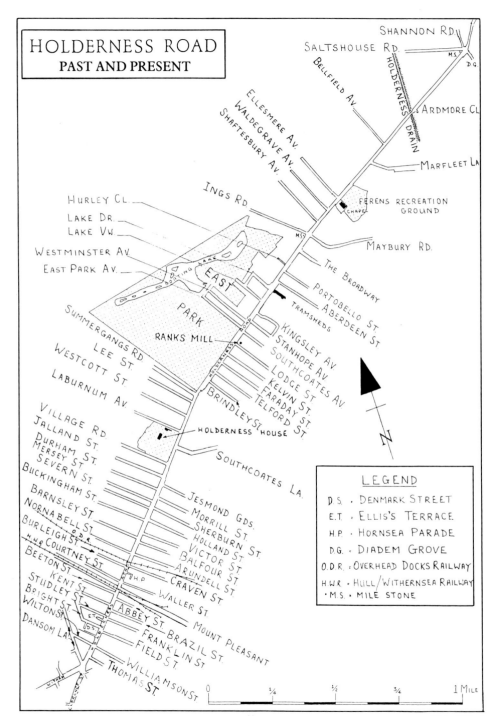

HOLDERNESS ROAD
PAST AND PRESENT

SHANNON RD.
SALTSHOUSE RD.
BELLFIELD AV.
HOLDERNESS DRAIN
ELLESMERE AV.
WALDEGRAVE AV.
SHAFTESBURY AV.
ARDMORE CL
MARFLEET LA
INGS RD.
HURLEY CL.
LAKE DR.
LAKE VW.
FERENS RECREATION GROUND
CHAPEL
M.S.
WESTMINSTER AV.
EAST PARK AV.
MAYBURY RD.
THE BROADWAY
PORTOBELLO ST.
EAST
BOATING LAKE
PARK
ABERDEEN ST.
TRAMSHEDS
SUMMERGANGS RD.
LEE ST.
WESTCOTT ST.
LABURNUM AV.
RANKS MILL
KINGSLEY AV.
STANHOPE AV.
SOUTHCOATES AV.
LODGE ST.
KELVIN ST.
FARADAY ST.
TELFORD ST.
VILLAGE RD.
JALLAND ST.
DURHAM ST.
MERSEY ST.
SEVERN ST.
BUCKINGHAM ST.
BARNSLEY ST.
NORNABELL ST.
BURLEIGH ST.
H.W.R. COURTNEY ST.
BEETON ST.
KENT ST.
STUDLEY ST.
BRIGHT ST.
WILTON ST.
DANSOM LA.
BRINDLEY ST.
HOLDERNESS HOUSE
SOUTHCOATES LA.
JESMOND GDS.
MORRILL ST.
SHERBURN ST.
HOLLAND ST.
VICTOR ST.
BALFOUR ST.
ARUNDELL ST.
CRAVEN ST.
WALLER ST.
O.D.R.
H.P.
ABBEY ST.
MOUNT PLEASANT
BRAZIL ST.
FRANKLIN ST.
FIELD ST.
E.T.
D.S.
WILLIAMSON ST.
THOMAS ST.

LEGEND

D.S. = DENMARK STREET
E.T. = ELLIS'S TERRACE
H.P. = HORNSEA PARADE
D.G. = DIADEM GROVE
O.D.R. = OVERHEAD DOCKS RAILWAY
H.W.R. = HULL/WITHERNSEA RAILWAY
·M.S.· = MILE STONE

N

0   ¼   ½   ¾   1 MILE

(*Michael Wilson*)

had been the Picturedrome from 1912 to 1928. The cinema was bombed in July 1941, along with the Hull Savings Bank at Franklin Street corner, so the frontage between the two streets was a pile of rubble with the gaunt empty end of the cinema where the balcony used to be towering over it all. People now walk into the Post Office just about where the cinema entrance was.

The **Savoy** at Morrill Street corner enjoyed full houses during the war and after, because the Ritz had gone and also the Sherburn in the same year. I believe the Savoy, which was opened in 1923, had some bomb damage in the last Hull raid of the war, the night of 17/18 March 1945, when high explosives were dropped in the Morrill Street/Holland Street area, a raid that caused a considerable number of fatal and other casualties. I do not remember if the cinema closed for repairs. It continued through the 1950s, but was then pulled down, taking with it a billiard hall and a couple of shops, to make way for Boyes' store which opened in 1961.

The **Astoria** building remains at the corner of Lake Drive looking as clean and handsome as it ever did. In the early 1930s the site was a grass paddock, with a simple low fence round it, the sort made of just one row of horizontal square timbers with their corners uppermost, strapped to small square posts, painted white. The interior of the new cinema seemed quite palatial, although it was simply designed and decorated, without the elaborations of earlier theatres. There was a multicoloured organ that went up and down, and murals on the walls of the stalls area — elephants on one side and tigers on the other. It opened in 1934, continued unscathed until well after the war and is now a bingo hall.

There was also, in Witham, the **Holderness Hall,** which still stands next to the Windmill Hotel. It opened the same year as the Ritz, a time when more people lived near the town. It was the **Gaumont** in 1950 but the general doldrums of the cinema industry and the awkwardness of its own position overtook it nine years later. It was soon re-opened as the **Majestic Ballroom,** attracting a younger clientèle for whom the distance was less trouble. Various pop groups entertained here, including, about 1960, a young Liverpudlian quartet billed small because they were as yet not very widely known. They were the Beatles.

Near the Crown Inn in 1910-11 was the East Park Roller Skating Rink. It may have been about the same site as the later T.A. Drill Hall (4th E.Yorks Regt.) as that was not completed until the summer of 1913. Another short-lived roller skating venue was at the corner of Holland Street, the East Hull Roller Skating Pavilion on Woolworth's site. The name hints that it could have been a temporary structure, perhaps even a marquee; in any case it was open for business only during 1910 and 1911, so the craze must have been short-lived — or the entrance charge too high!

Until the start of the 1989-90 season, on certain afternoons and evenings a stranger would have thought there was only one form of leisure on Holderness Road, judging by the orderly crowds of people of all ages, men and women, wearing red and white scarves and favours of the Robins, Hull Kingston Rovers Rugby League Club. Rugby football was established on Holderness Road in the 1870s, as the Hull Rugby Football Club, formed in 1865, although not itself of East Hull origin, amalgamated with what had 'graduated' from an East Hull junior club, the Hull White Star. The merger took place in 1881 and the resulting club played under Union rules at a new, well-appointed ground that had its East stand backing on to the Brunswick Chapel and the opposite stand where Severn Street now is, until the move to the Boulevard at the end of the 1894-5 season.

Meanwhile, a group of local youths, late teenagers for the most part, formed themselves into the Kingston Amateurs, becoming Kingston Rovers, a senior team, in the late 1880s when they played on a variety of grounds in West Hull, including the Boulevard, before choosing a home in Craven Street in 1895. There followed for all clubs a time when rules were changed regarding both the game itself and the players' standing and Rugby League emerged from what had been Rugby Union. Hull F.C. therefore was a West Hull club from the start of the League and Rovers were by then in the eastern part of the town. Rovers continued in Craven Street until the 1922-3 season when the £18,281 purchase, Craven Park, came into use.

One of the openings from Holderness Road is called Wilkinson Avenue. I was told it was named after Jack Wilkinson, a former player, but there are coincidences regarding this bit of land. In 1848 it was owned by George Wilkinson who had been dealing in land and owned other plots on Holderness Road and elsewhere. There were the two Wilkinsons, J. H. and J. R., players in the first Craven Park season in which Rovers won the League Championship and also, in the years before the First World War, W. E. Wilkinson and Son, Estate Agents, at the shop where the East Park Post Office now is next to Wilkinson Avenue itself.

The Mersey Street ground was taken for building pretty soon after Hull F.C. left, but the newly formed Hull Brunswick A.F.C. (1894) may have used the pitch close to the chapel for a little while before going to the grounds on Holderness Road near the later Wesleyan Chapel opposite Ellesmere Avenue. Brunswick continued in amateur status for 79 years, finally disbanding in 1973. It was one of the products of the social or educational side of Brunswick's activities, one of its founder members being J. T. Ferens. The club was variously known as Brunswick Wesleyan, then from 1902 the Brunswick Institute, and latterly Brunswick A.F.C., but, whatever the name, the team acquitted themselves well throughout.

Rovers, too, have gone from Holderness Road. After sharing the Craven Park ground with greyhound racing since February 1941, they moved in 1989 to Poorhouse Lane on Greatfield, a matter of heartache for some for whom Craven Park was the only possible home for the Robins.

rance, East Park, Hull.

East Park is the great pleasure-ground of Holderness Road. Following a much earlier suggestion by Ald. Hodge, 52 acres of land were laid out as a park, to be opened on the day of Queen Victoria's Golden Jubilee, 21 June 1887, and was thus Hull's third park after Pearson's and West Park. The *Hull Daily Mail* reporting at this time on the miseries of unemployment, even though the preparation of East Park was in a way an early job-creation scheme, said of the forthcoming Jubilee in general: '... the Jubilee celebration in Hull is a miserable fiasco ... Beyond the opening of the Market Hall and the East Park, which are after all the veriest formalities, nothing in the shape of sight-seeing has been provided to relieve the monotony of daily life ... Nothing but rain is needed to complete the misery of the Jubilee celebrations.' Nevertheless, two days later, on 22 June 1887, the tone was rather less dismal: 'Long before two o'clock on Monday, large crowds of persons took up every vantage point in Lowgate and other streets through which the demonstration was to pass on the way to East Park.' The report describes how, headed by the police band, carriage-loads of civic dignitaries set off from the Town Hall, Lowgate, and in Savile Street were joined by the Knights of the Golden Horn in their dazzling uniforms, children from the Spring Bank Orphan Home, followed by two rullies carrying employees of the Blind Institute making baskets en route, and then contingents of Druids, Oddfellows and Foresters. At the park, the chairman of the Parks Committee presented a casket to the mayor who then declared the park, with its eight acres set aside for cricket, football, *etc.*, officially open.

This first phase of the park was entered through the fine iron gates that were sent off to help the war effort in 1939 or '40; the horse chestnuts of the entrance avenue and the limes further down were planted; there were lawns and shrubberies, as one might expect, and, later, the large greenhouse or conservatory that was a magnet for Sunday afternoon strollers right up to the time of the Blitz. The model yacht pond was also an early popular feature, as was the bandstand. There was a winding ornamental lake, delighting the Victorian sense of the picturesque, and the artificial hills and cliffs made bridges necessary and therefore viewpoints were created. The horse trams came up to Lee Street from the town and as the flat rate fare for any journey was just one penny (1d) many people from other parts of the town availed themselves of the fresh air and beauty of the park.

In 1913 T. R. Ferens gave an additional tract of land, largely for a boating lake. By that time the brickworks at the Willows and behind Westminster Avenue stretched back almost to the Summergangs Dike, and the (now) James Reckitt Avenue side of the park lake is roughly on the line of the dike, curving sharply where the houses re-commence after the gap opposite Malet Lambert School because here the Summergangs Dike and the Lambwath Stream joined. The brickponds were incorporated into the lake and paddling pool, although made shallower. The ceremony to inaugurate the lake and park extension was brief, Mr. Ferens presenting the gift and the mayor accepting it. A procession of boats led by the Kingston Rowing Club went out on the lake, while the assembled company was served afternoon tea.

The Thirties was still a time of Sunday afternoon walks, strolls through the greenhouses and a pause by the aviary, another innovation of 1913. For interest, too, as well as its preservation the 'old watchtower' as it was called, the bartizan from the south-west corner of the Citadel near Sammy's Point, had been built into the retaining wall of some of the park's higher ground, on the suggestion of Sir Albert Rollitt, and not far from this was the bandstand. Regular and superb displays of flowers were set out by the park staff and it was a 'must' to go in due season to see the bank of dahlias at the back of the bowling green or to view the floral clock to the left of the main avenue. Many a housewife spent a few minutes during morning shopping on a walk through the Tower Grange greenhouse, especially when the spring bulbs or the chrysanthemums were on show. A small golf course set out in the field behind Ings Road was popular just before the war. The park was a happy, wholesome place to be.

During the war a barrage balloon was on the tennis courts behind the Willows pond, the greenhouses were severely damaged and park staffing reduced. I believe that the dahlia bank was converted to vegetables, but am not sure of this. The park has not regained its former horticultural glory, but has remained an important pleasure ground, the venue for organised firework displays, the end point of the Lord Mayor's Parade and for other carnivals. The Police Station took the land where were the Tower Grange greenhouses, including a large range of nursery glasshouses and outside beds where the plants were reared. Changes in the original park's layout were made necessary by wartime neglect: Khyber Pass lost its bridge and also the doors that had been copied from an Arab doorway in Zanzibar to form the entrance to the African Pavilion in the 1928 Wembley Exhibition. The open air swimming ponds, one for boys (1913) and one for girls (1920s), were replaced by the Lido in 1964; then the Woodford Centre for a variety of healthy activities was opened on Holderness Road opposite Rank's old mill in April 1982.

Visitors to East Park now share it with vast flocks of geese, Canada, greylag and others, which are a mixed blessing. They inhabit the north-easterly part of the park, cropping the grass and sometimes taking over the area near the boats, with a fairly benign attitude toward human visitors, but leaving a lot of filth on the walkways. Other wild life can be seen including magpies, kestrels and grey squirrels, even on a brisk walk through the park. Without doubt other species are there for the careful observer, as it is a large green area in a city that has gradually surrounded it during its century of existence.

THE LATE THIRTIES

Fifty years on is a justified time for looking back, even for some nostalgia. With a complete list before me of all the occupants of Holderness Road in the years just before the war, to give accuracy to my memories, I find that some names, places and people are more readily called to mind than others. So this is definitely a personal selection.

I lived 'beyond tram ends', that is, beyond where the trams and later trolley-buses turned round at Ings Road, the former city boundary. Even in those days the road beyond, generally called Holderness High Road, seemed wider than the rest; it may have been because some of the 1920s houses were set fairly well back and even in the case of Nos. 881, 883, 891 and 893 had railed-off short front gardens with a grass plot between the garden and the pavement in anticipation of road-widening.

There were mature trees here and there; some poplars on the line of the Summergangs Dyke next to the garden of East-Thorpe at Maybury Road corner; a fairly large copper beech in the front garden of No. 810; and a row of magnificent black poplars in the paddock opposite Waldegrave Avenue. These were not the straight Lombardy variety, but graceful, fluid trees which shimmered in the wind and in due season covered the ground with dark red catkin-like flowers and later with cotton-wool. Glen Helen had

Traces of past employment.   Top: A cowkeeper's cottage in Marfleet Lane. It was demolished in 1945. Below: The remains of claypits behind The Willows, now a haven for fishermen, once a busy brickworks.

Lombardy poplars down the sides and across the front, with other smaller trees and shrubs between. An old ash guarded the entrance to the Brunswick playing field next to the Wesleyan Chapel and there was a high old hawthorn hedge screening the field from the road. Spring was on its way when the blackthorn came into flower at the corner of Marfleet Lane.

At Ings Road corner on the north side of the road was Fussey's farm. It faced the main road, but, as with most farmsteads, the back door was always used and the address was therefore No. 2, Ings Road. There was a fair sized garden occupying the corner, regularly set out with vegetables and cottage garden flowers; I particularly remember the lupins. Near the outbuildings on Ings Road were a few fruit trees and others; the story goes that a large branch or billet was dug up when the Crooked Billet's foundations were being laid, hence the name. A narrow strip of paddock beside the farm was taken into the pub grounds when it was built in 1967; this was next to No. 809.

The Hull Co-op shops at the corner of Shaftesbury Avenue always seemed odd, an intrusion, as they were very solidly built and of three storeys, providing living accommodation above. In the mid-Thirties other shops appeared on this stretch of road. As had happened elsewhere, dwellings were turned into shops and very strange it seemed to me, never having seen it happen before. These shops were at Nos. 869-873 (four of the six known as Leyland Villas) and included Norah Smith's greengrocery, Mr. Soare's shoe repairing business, Stan V. Oliver, butcher, and the Misses Wood who were pastrycooks and also sold some groceries and dairy products. I vaguely remember Nos. 875-7-9 being built in the early or mid-Thirties and then there were slightly older houses, including Mr Needler's Calderstones, before the open fields were reached. There was a good wide ditch along the roadside and an ancient hawthorn hedgerow. The side of the path was high with 'bad man's oatmeal' in June, and birds such as waxwings came to feed on the abundant haws on the hedge in winter. Haldenby's (Ings House) was another house that looked like a farmstead, but which had been a mill house. It was set very well back and provided a space next to the old Four-in-Hand, and later the space made parking for the new pub of 1937.

There were more fields with their old hedgerows at the other side of Bellfield Avenue, then Wright's (Salt Ings Farm) before the drain and Wray's just past it. There were outbuildings at Wray's, another typical small Holderness farmhouse, brick with a pantile roof. In the late Thirties Mr Wray was no longer a cowkeeper, but bought milk and re-sold it. We put a basin out each morning, he delivered the milk from a metal churn and I believe he would make a second, afternoon delivery in hot weather. By the beginning of the war a few houses had been built between Wray's and Saltshouse Lane as it was then called. These were Nos. 1143-5, 1151-3 and 1169-1183 and at first they had fields in between. At Saltshouse Lane was a farm with its stackyard on the corner, behind it Eastfield House with a drive leading down to the lodge on the main road on the town side of the farm. Here were trees, many of them sycamores, with a scatter of snowdrops under them in the spring.

The south side of the road was filled with buildings almost the whole way from the Brunswick Recreation Ground to beyond the Saltshouse junction. Although of many different styles, built over a period of years from about 1905 to 1925, these houses present a unified picture of middle-class gentility, the suburbs of their time, the beginning of the ribbon development that some years later started again in Bilton Village and continued past Wyton Bar. Most of these on Holderness High Road were semi-detached family houses but there were a few individually designed single ones. The bungalow was just coming into vogue and there are three similar ones at Nos. 894-6-8. The bungalow at No. 900 is different and used to be called Lu-Helan. It was the home of Miss L. Hewitt, partner of the firm of Hewitt and Thompson, bakers and confectioners, which flourished across the time of the First World War. Miss Hewitt was Lou or Lu, her partner, Helan, hence the name.

House names were used a great deal in this district of Sutton Ings up to the last war, as the city boundary had altered only in 1929 and before that this part of the road was in Sutton parish without the benefit of town numbering. And what names there were! Sardomene, One Ash (but where was the ash?), Aver Rajah where Captain Coysh lived, and No. 831 with Glaisdale in gold lettering on the glass above the door, but called St. Amant by everybody when talking of it. Legend had it that this house was built by, or bought by, someone who had won money on a horse called St. Amant and, sure enough, in the list of Derby winners is a horse of that name, owned by L. Rothschild, winner in 1914, the year the house was built. Many letters were delivered to our house with the meagre address 'Brockholme, Sutton Ings'. Marfleet Lane still had the appearance of a country lane and it, like the main road, was lit by gas lamps, although in the lane they were few and along one side only.

At the corner opposite St. Michael's Church was Whitfield's old farmstead (Sutton Ings Farm) with a garden in front and large yard with outbuildings at the back. Mr Edwin Whitfield, who, I was told, had been one of the youngest skippers in the Gamecock Fleet, was by this time a tallow-chandler and carried on the smelly business of boiling tallow in this nice suburban area until after the Second World War. Whitfield's farm was overhung by some ancient elms and there were also elm trees in the front gardens of several houses beyond the drain bridge. Old stumps of them can still be seen as some of them survived only to be stricken with Dutch elm disease in more recent years.

Opposite the Saltshouse junction in the 1930s was a garage and petrol pump to cater for the growing number of cars. This was Rusling's, later Jubilee, Garage, a tin shack just past the coach house of Craiglands, now

Mr. Cox stands at the right of the group with his wife and assistants in front of what was arguably one of the best fish shops in Hull. The season was just before Easter; the year, the mid- or late-1930s. Cod 4d per lb; skate 8d; and look at that halibut!

(Picture courtesy of Mr. A. B. Pougher)

Apollo Club, the large house owned by Richard Finch, builder. At the back of these was a triangular field that had been a chicken farm briefly in the late 1920s, and further back a number of fields of apparently poor quality land.

Beyond the tram ends the only transport service was the EYMS, with buses to Aldbrough, Preston, Hornsea (by various routes), Bridlington and Swine. Most people, except the businessmen going to and from work, walked from Bellfield Avenue or Marfleet Lane to the tram and later the trolley-bus; certainly this was the practice for most women when shopping, even for many who lived beyond the drain bridge.

The Parade, between Lake Drive and Lake View, with other shops in that locality, provided almost all that was commonly needed: confectioners (Smith's, later Reed and Mackman); fish (Ted Cox); greengrocery (Noble's); sweets and tobacco (Zeta); and drapery (Mrs Dean) were among the Parade shops and there were also two grocers' shops nearby (Hart's and Bourne's, each with an errand lad); Argenta, William Allison and Fairbank, three butchers; the East Park Post Office a few doors from its present position; more sweets and tobacco at Mrs Cooper's next to the tramsheds (enormous ice-cream cornets, ha'penny each); a pet shop and cycle dealer in the same block; Taylor's fish and chips at the other side of the tramsheds, and, near to the Willows, Mrs Ditchburn's drapery store, a house-front shop.

A sign of the times was the electrical shop of E. Arthur Gale at the corner of Aberdeen Street. In the late Thirties many people began using electricity instead of gas for lighting the home and once electricity was installed they could also use portable electric fires, electric irons and kettles. A new trade of electrician or electrical engineer had been created, but the older one of plumber still carried on in the same way. Several plumbers were listed on Holderness Road in 1939 (H. B. Leng, C. F. Proctor, E. Robinson and T. Cawkill) but as yet none of them called themselves plumber and electrician. As well as Mr Gale's shop there was Turner Bros., Electrical Engineers, opposite Jesmond Gardens. Both of these dealt in radios, but already there were H. W. Downes, Louis Moseson, Ernest Kendrick and Charles Stromberg advertising as wireless dealers or suppliers. As for the other major modern innovation, the car, as part of the lives of ordinary people, that was hardly catered for at all. The Jubilee Filling Station where Diadem Grove now is, F. W. Scott, motor engineer near Jesmond Gardens and the Paragon Motor Co. at the corner of East Park Avenue were between them sufficient to meet the needs of the Holderness Road motorists. By this time the 'Allo Motor and Engineering Co. had been overtaken by the Jesmond Recreation club.

A penny fare took one to the Durham Street stage from Ings Road and about here the major density of shops began. Not that the road was one continual line of shops, even in the Thirties; quite a number of private houses remained with vestigial front gardens, usually of derelict privet bushes, and some of these remained as residential property into the 1980s. Some of these houses were doctors' surgeries; for example, Dr E. Alderson in Wilton Terrace, Dr Egan next to the Public Benefit, in a house which still exists as the Whistling Kettle café and which had a long history of occupancy by various doctors right back to the 1880s; Drs G. McDougall and G. Yule at No. 168, one of the old grey brick houses of Hornsea Parade, set back between later shops, a house where Dr Hollingworth had been since the end of the last century. There was also Max Adler, dentist, in a bay-windowed house, one of Myrtle Villas near Arundel Street. Further out along the road the surgery of F. Stamford Brittan, dentist, was swallowed up by the post-war development which created the Grandways Supermarket opposite Summergangs Road, although the former house premises of Mr Potter, dentist, now has a shop front and no garden and is still in the family as Raymond M. Potter, Optometrist.

During the Thirties the jostle for main road positions by the chain stores had begun, but not the chains we think of today. Then, when wages were low and, at the start of the decade at least, many breadwinners were unemployed, the tightest competition between shops was among those that sold foodstuffs. Lipton's, Maypole, Home and Colonial were three of the most usual names of food shops to be seen on the main roads of many towns, and in the Hull area also William Jackson and Son Ltd. and William Cussons, the latter also having drapery departments.

Between the level crossing and the overhead bridge, the narrowest part of the road with a hinterland of terrace houses in Craven, Courtney, Burleigh and Waller Streets, were Lipton's (No. 145), John S. Driver (No. 155), Home and Colonial next, then the Argenta Meat Co. Next was Fred Key, butcher, followed by British Traders, grocers, and the Meadow Dairy Co., another grocery. Maypole was two doors away at No. 171 and between Meadow and Maypole were two of the early clothing chains, Fleming Reid and Co., hosiers (later called the Scotch Wool Shop) and Wyles Bros., boot factors, who already had other shops along this road and other roads of the city. Cussons had both grocery and drapery at the corner of Thomas Street and a grocery department at the corner of Barnsley Street; Jackson's were at Bright Street corner and they also had a large, purpose-built row of shops at the corner of Mersey Street and another, three-storeyed and elaborate, at the corner of Southcoates Avenue.

Meanwhile the Hull Co-op competed with all of them in stores near Holland Street, another a few yards from the Crown Inn and a third at the corner of Shaftesbury Avenue. However, this was long past the time when the manager of Holderness Road's first Co-op, at the corner of Wilton Street, would stop incoming country carriers' carts and buy butter *etc.* for sale in the shop. Other local firms that by this time had a fair number of shops in Hull and district selling goods of basic types were Mallory's Hardware with 11 shops in Hull, also Alfred Smith and Son, bakers and pork butchers, and the rival firm of J. J. N. Mackman Ltd.

Individual shops flourished, among them a number of gown shops and milliners. Women had plenty of choice, for Ingram's, opposite East Park gates, sold dresses as well as underwear in their Ladies' department; there were Dorothea Turner under the Savoy cinema, Kitty Blaxland in the block at the other side of Morrill Street, and, perhaps the best-remembered of them all, Lottie Miller at No. 339 next door to Durham Villa. On the parade of shops near St Columba's Church, Minnie Cox had a milliner's shop and there was also Thompson and Lunn at No. 289. These were not the 'fashion shops' of today; they — and others — sold high-quality goods that were stylish and lasting.

Other specialist shops of a completely different type were the tripe dressers. At No. 129, just by the railway line, was a tiny shop, Pedder's, a Mecca for those who liked the slithery delicacy. Another tripe dresser was Harold Ramsey at No. 251 near the Elephant and Castle, another small shop, too, for the premises were shared with H. H. Bennet, butcher.

Especially as employment increased with the imminence of World War

Two, the brief period between the Coronation of George VI and the autumn of 1939 seemed in my recollection to be a boom time. Particularly on Saturday afternoons people walked the length of the road window-shopping and buying, rather than going into the town where some things were more expensive. Woolworth's opened for business (strictly 3d and 6d only) on 24 September 1937, the smallwares and cheap goods displayed on open counters as we are accustomed to seeing them today. At certain other shops goods were to hand, as, for example, the more bulky items at Mallory's and on the forecourts of some of the fruit shops, especially where the former front gardens of Victorian houses had been concreted over after the conversion to shops, as between Nornabell and Buckingham Streets, on both sides of the road. Free-standing glass display cases were a feature of some forecourts: for example, Horace Cripps' toys and fancy goods and Ainley's, gentlemen's outfitters. The former was very dusty and, I suspect, unchanged, but at Ainley's there was always an immaculate display, often of men's shirt collars.

Although the mills had long since ceased to operate and most of them were demolished, there was still the trade of corn factor. Hesk's had an office and yard between the railway and Beeton Street, while Lorrimar's business was at the site of, and probably in some of the original outbuildings of the Anti-mill near Balfour Street, with Grasby's at Craven Street corner near the overhead bridge.

Another relic was the pawnbroker's sign. Five pawnbrokers were listed on the main road for 1939; they were Owen and Robinson's on Wilton Terrace, Chas. Turner at No. 85 between Studley and Kent Streets, two shops of Eric V. Manham, and Joseph Goldman, listed at his residence near Southcoates Lane. This was the darker side of what I judged as cheerful crowds of shoppers before the war. It matched the old women wearing men's caps or with black shawls over their heads and the barefoot children who were a great contrast to the crowds of workers, many of them girls, leaving Reckitt's at five o'clock or Saturday dinnertimes and the dirty but employed workmen whose bicycles filled the roadway waiting those interminable minutes for the level crossing to open.

In 1939, of the Big Five banks, four — Barclay's, Midland, Lloyd's and National Provincial — had premises on the road, only Westminster being absent. Branches of the Hull Savings Bank were at the corners of Franklin Street and Southcoates Lane and there was also the Yorkshire Penny Bank near Arundel Street. There were no building societies and the only estate agent listed was Dacre and Son at No. 443A. Since Wood Grange (by then occupied by the Christian Scientists) was next door and No. 443 was Canon Berry's home at Drypool Vicarage near Lee Street, No. 443A must have been a building, maybe temporary, on the site of Turnberry Court.

There were eight fish and chip shops between Windmill corner and the city boundary in 1939, compared with five today; four, at Nos. 327, 624 and

720 (now owned by Cyril Crimlis), and No. 741 (now K. & R. Bourne) had carried on the same trade in the same premises since the 1920s. Chow Mein and pizzas were unheard of on Holderness Road at that time.

Before the Blitz, then, there was a rich diversity of small shops; the road was a robust, active, friendly place, a long narrow market town which drew people from their own 'villages' in the side streets.

WORLD WAR TWO

The devastation and dislocation caused by the bombing of World War Two are not to be measured merely by the number of gaps in the Victorian terraces, nor the obviously modern buildings which complete rows of shops that have earlier features. Only recently have some of the gaps been filled with shop units of the style of the time, not just the plainly functional War Damage repairs. The two rows of shops at the corner of Buckingham and Severn Streets are of the late 1980s and offer a somewhat different appearance from their predecessors. Only in the past few years, also, has an attempt been made to incorporate Holderness Road into a city-wide network of roads linking with the motorway beyond the city and avoiding the inevitably slow passage through the centre.

First, what happened in the war.

Canon Berry, Vicar of Drypool, 1914-1947, regarded his parish as the most bombed in the most bombed town in England. The estuary provided a wonderful guideline for the raiders and the people of East Hull, recalling what the Zeppelins had done to Clarence and Waller Streets in June, 1915, anticipated in some measure the horror that was to come. Outright and instant demolition was caused by high explosive bombs, and fires from relatively small incendiary bombs severely damaged many buildings; scarcely a house or other building escaped damage from the blast both of enemy explosives and our own anti-aircraft fire. Today a remarkable number of Victorian and Edwardian buildings remain along the road; tidied up and mended, with new shop fronts, their appearance does not reveal to the unknowing observer that most of them had windows shattered, roof slates dislodged, door and window frames wrenched out, and ceilings and walls cracked or brought down by the blast.

The following are places where buildings were either totally destroyed or so badly damaged that they had to be pulled down: in the middle of Wilton Terrace; the Crystal sales area, the site of one of Hull's worst incidents, a land-mine on a public air raid shelter in Ellis's Terrace; corner of Beeton Street, the Southcoates Station Hotel; next to the overhead bridge where the police 'box' now is; near Nornabell Street in front of the high flats (another land-mine); between Barnsley and Buckingham Streets where now (1990) building is in progress, where a prefab. office has been for many years; in front of Buckingham Street School; the corner of Severn Street; two of the shops near Jalland Street; St. Columba's Church; all but one of the parade

Spot the difference! Two of these shops near Jalland Street were rebuilt after 1945, but the fact is not noticed at shop-window level.

One shop stands forward of the parade near Westcott Street, the only one remaining after bombing. The post-war rebuilt shops were set back in anticipation of road widening.

of shops near the church; Westcott House; semi-detached houses near Minster Court beyond Holderness Drain bridge where three parachute mines became entangled and came down together; property near the English Presbyterian Church where a packaging firm now is; the Hull Savings Bank at the corner of Franklin Street; the Ritz cinema at the corner of Brazil Street and one of the row of shops at the other corner of the street; shops near Victor Street; Woolworth's; Prospect House where the Co-op Funeral Service now is; Wilton House; the end of the row, now Mascarade; shops, dwellings in the gap which forms Grandways car-park; and many other buildings close to, but not directly on, Holderness Road itself.

After a heavy raid, jagged pieces of shrapnel from anti-aircraft shells were found on the streets and sometimes there were small magnesium bombs that had been extinguished with sand-bags. The Holderness High Road parachute mine incident covered the road with lumps of clay as far as Marfleet Lane end; they had been spewed out of the two enormous craters made by the explosions. The evening after the first May blitz in 1941, a clear warm evening, saw Holderness Road as truly a route into Holderness, for in lorries provided by the Chief Air Raid Warden, R. G. Tarran, on bicycles and on foot was a procession of refugees from the wrath to come, as people left their homes and made for the comparative safety of farm and field beyond the city boundary.

Moods after the war were as mixed as the interests to be served. An opportunity to provide better working-class housing seemed to have presented itself and the aim of the authorities was, as quickly as possible, to re-house the bombed-out families and the returning servicemen in dwellings that had modern amenities within the space and air around them. The first solution was the pre-fabricated house, developed during the latter part of the war to ensure that a large number of new homes could be produced in the shortest possible time. A group of pre-fabs was built in fields going up to the Four-in-Hand; they were arranged in small lanes end-on to the road.

It was about the only possible site for them on the main road, and indeed there was little room for immediate inner-city domestic development, despite all the bombing, even if anybody wanted to stay close to the city centre. So the pre-war projection of Bilton Grange (where many of the roads had already been constructed across a flat featureless area of fairly unproductive land) became a reality and Longhill Estate was built in the early 1950s from Saltshouse Road to the city boundary. Longhill was planned sympathetically, using the lines of former hedgerows for its winding main road, Shannon Road, and retaining some mature trees in the process. By 1970, however, with the more far-reaching Bransholme scheme under way, many people had tucked themselves back into the familiar little patched-up terraces of Courtney Street and elsewhere and did not wish to go to the wide-open and unknown peripheral estates. Their old houses, many

*Rows of prefabs were built end-on to the main road opposite Marfleet Lane. The Rington's tea cart
passes by at the dispersal of the 1971 Lord Mayor's Parade.*

of two-up, two-down sham-four variety, were being pulled down by the
score and the hinterland of Holderness Road in many sections became
empty or sparse of dwellings. This in turn had its effect on the appearance
of the main road, as such staple shops as grocers, butchers and drapers
thinned out still further, more noticeably than occurred in the reduction of
immediate post-war years. The practice of the proprietor's family living
over the shop had also dwindled as some of the upper floors had become
barely habitable anyway, certainly according to the higher standards
expected in post-war times.

In this respect the war had violently accelerated a change that had already
been noted in the 1930s, for in the *1938 Methodist Conference Handbook* was
a comment that Kingston Chapel in Witham was 'less favourably situated
than of old because of the receding tide of population'. Although the chapel
'refused to become a down-town cause', traders in the area of Witham and
Holderness Road nearest to the town were compelled to move out. The
1950s, the so-called period of austerity, left much of Holderness Road in
sorry plight, with empty shops, derelict upper floors and roughly-cleared
gaps between buildings where bombed rubble had been taken away and
nothing much else done. To be fair, the task facing Hull was a massive one
and it was being attempted when an 'off with the old, on with the new'
feeling was prevalent among some people who wanted to pull down and start

from scratch while others had a longing to 'let's get back to normal, back to the old ways'.

The Abercrombie Plan of 1945 admitted, when referring to the city centre, that 'bombing, ironically enough, has not provided a sufficiently "clean sheet" to permit a more optimistic programme of rebuilding'. This, as has already been implied, was the case with Holderness Road. The Plan, however, was not the Official Development Plan for post-war Hull, and the powers that would have been needed to put it into operation were not provided until the Town and Country Planning Act (1947). Even so, Abercrombie's ideas were seen as an easily-understood example of bold planning and therefore provoked a great deal of discussion and argument. Apart from the need to cope with the problem of war damage, the improvement of living conditions in many areas was long overdue, even in 1939, but some of the measures that were taken after the war had a distinctly *ad hoc* look to them, as the official Development Plan for the city was not approved by the Ministry of Housing and Local Government until 1954.

In addition, no-one could foresee the revolution in transport that would take place so quickly. Where in the 1930s and 40s the workforce went to work on foot, on trams or trolley-buses and overwhelmingly by bicycle, and the railway to Withernsea and to goods terminals regularly provided a barrier to road transport at the level crossing, within no time, it seemed, the rail links had gone (1967) and the road was full of cars and other motor vehicles.

A 1937 census of delays at Hull level crossings, given in the Abercrombie Report, shows that on 23 January 1937 at the Holderness Road crossing, 62 trains passed through and the gates were closed for a total of 1 hour 45 minutes. Some closures allowed more than one train to pass so that in the 15 hours in which the count was made that day, the gates closed 56 times for an average of 1.9 minutes each. The census gave the number of 'units' passing through the level crossing and it needs no modern comparative sample to show the change in road usage to the present time:

Pedestrians 1,454
Cycles   563
Vehicles   382 — this would include horse-drawn carts and rullies.

However great the change may seem now from the old congested stretch of Holderness Road between the overhead bridge and the level crossing when compared with the new wide intersection of Mount Pleasant and a more open Holderness Road, the recommendations of the Abercrombie Plan were even bolder in their scope. North and south orbital links were envisaged, the former to join up with Hessle Road from Windmill corner, the road being taken over the river by means of a high-level, non-opening bridge with a gradient of 1 in 30; the south orbital link, again from Windmill corner, would require another slope to reach a second river bridge, this gradient being along the line of Witham, descending at the other side to the eastern end of Jarratt Street to a new railway station. With the removal of the level crossings by extended use of existing and proposed high-level railways, Holderness Road would have been radically changed. (As it proved, the remedy was more radical as the root cause of level crossing delay, the trains themselves, were removed.) This was not all, for in the road's hinterland would have been other developments greatly altering the usage of the road by vehicles and pedestrians. An electric tramway was proposed to link the city with a new Burton Constable satellite town and providing also a link with Hedon Road by means of a road with tramway from the Ganstead roundabout. A technical school was planned for Lake Drive!

As with all large scale town planning, it could not be organic, despite phasing the development over periods of years; the changes of attitudes could not be foreseen, nor the post-war population boom. However, a bold overall view by a competent outsider puts any human problem into new perspective whether the proffered advice be taken or not. This was the case with the Abercrombie Plan; the diversity of factors mitigating against it were legion. Had it been put into operation, many more of the features of Holderness Road that tell us something of the people who passed this way before us would have been swept away.

No. 1 Holderness Road in 1968, apart from the shop-fronts remarkably little changed since being built in the 1850s.

HOLDERNESS ROAD PANORAMA, 1990 — FROM ONE END OF THE ROAD TO THE OTHER

South side

Nos 2, 4, 6 (brick, with wrought iron 'dome')	After Clarence Street cut through in 1902.
Former Gas Showrooms	After Clarence Street cut through in 1902.
Gap	Part of Blockhouse Mill yard.
No. 16	
Gap	Cobbled entrance to mill yard.
Nos 20-24	
26 and 30, Southcoat's; 28, Hull and Sculcoates Dispensary	1929, site of 1851 Model Houses.
Thomas Street	Before 1853.
Nos 34, 36	
Nos 38-44 and 58-52	Somerstown, first mentioned in *Baines' Directory*, 1823.
No. 46	'Modern' insertion into Somerstown.
Williamson Street	A street there unnamed, 1834. As South Parade, there in 1842.
3 shops, bay windows above	East Parade, first mentioned as East Parade, Somerstown, 1823.
No. 58 and Green Man	Built into shell of former Presbyterian Church of 1874. Point of roof above Green Man entrance, built 1980s.
Blank wall and Tony Britton, packaging	After World War 2, probably 1960s.
Field Street	As Prospect Place, there in 1834, called Field Street by 1861.
Shops (9) original houses set back 3-4 yards from shop fronts	Extension of East Parade.
Cobbled carriage arch	
No. 84, bay window above shop	Extension of East Parade.
James Reckitt Public Library	1889, first stone laid 9 April 1889.
East Hull Baths	Opened 1 October 1898.
Nos. 94, 96	
Franklin Street	First directory entry 1895, could be between 1890 and 1895.
T.S.B. site	Site of Stockton House (Francis Reckitt) then Drypool Vicarage, sold to Hull Savings Bank, 1893. Rebuilt after World War 2 bombing. Bank closed 1989, demolished August 1990.

Post Office	On site of Ritz cinema, bombed July 1941.
Brazil Street	After 1890. First directory entry 1895.
Gap	Bombed, July 1941.
Row of 3-storey shops, 116-126, (6, were 7)	1890s.
Housemartin Housing Association flats	1987, on site of St Andrew's Church.
Abbey Street	About 1892, at first from Williamson Street only, not to Holderness Road until after 1900.
Holderness Road Steam Mill	1838. In 1990 being coverted into an hotel, the Corn Mill Hotel.
Mount Pleasant	1988 on the line of the railway.
Car sales	1988.
Gap	Robert's Terrace, Nag's Head, Waller Street, shops formerly Cottage Row, Hornsea Parade demolished for road-works 1988.
Craven Park public house	Converted from Hornsea Villa which was there in 1851.
Shop	1989.
Shops, Craven Street corner	
Craven Street	As Marfleet Lane, there before 1851. Renamed 1878.
Gap	Demolished after 1970.
Overhead bridge	1885.
4 shops	Were Owthorne Villas, there 1889.
Yorkshire Bank	
Arundel Street	Between 1872 and 1881.
Shops (4)	Were Myrtle Villas, there 1889.
Presto Supermarket	On site of former shops but was frontage to land connected with the Anti-mill built 1795.
Balfour Fisheries No. 220	Fills the opening to the mill yard.
Corner Balfour Street	About 1895.
Balfour Street	First directory entry 1895.
Shops (10)	First directory entry 1895.
Victor Street	First directory entry 1895.
Nos. 246, 248, 250 (Skelton's; Boot's)	Post-World War 2 rebuild.
Nos. 258, 260, 262, 264	1890s. Waddingham's mill was here.
Gateway Supermarket	1960s on site of former Co-op.
Holland Street	Late 1890s.

Woolworth's building	In 1989 part converted to T.S.B. Woolworth's opened 24 September 1937; bombed; restored; closed January 1989.
Nos. 286, 288, 290, 292 Shops, gabled, 3-storey (5)	There as houses 1901, except for (then) Post Office, Sherburn Street corner.
Sherburn Street	Shown as projection on 1889 OS. Not a through road until after 1890.
Shops (5)	All one build, houses originally, there about 1901.
Boyes' Store	On site of Savoy cinema; Boyes built 1961.
Morrill Street	There as Hodge Avenue 1892. No through road until after 1900.
Shops Former entrance lane to East Hull Clinic Iceland Freezer shop, No. 324	Site of Durham House, there before 1872, used as TB Dispensary from before World War 1. Shop built 1980s.
Shops to corner	After 1921.
Jesmond Gardens	Between 1914 and 1919.
Jesmond Club	May have been site of Carmen's Buildings, 1861, as Brooke's ware-house behind it was Hull Street Tramway Co's Stables.
Nos. 330, 332	Linden Villa and Albany House, there in 1889.
No. 334	There 1889.
Nos. 336, 340	Glenmore Villas, there in 1889.
Co-op. Undertakers	Site of Prospect House. Post-World War 2.
Pramland	Shop built on to front of Saxby House, once home of T. R. Ferens; house was there in 1889.
Woodlands (Barnado's)	Was there 1889.
9 shops formerly houses	Were called Pleasant Place, there 1889.
Shops (Sparkles etc.)	Site of H. P. Darling's Nursery green-house, marked on 1889 OS.
Hare's greengrocers	1990.
Wallis pork butcher etc. (382-4-6)	More of Pleasant Place.
Nos. 388, 390, 392, 394	
Nos. 396, 398, 400 with gables	Woodside Villas.

Southcoates Lane	As Southcoates Road on 1853 OS but track existed before that.
T.S.B.	On site of York House, there 1889. Bank, early 20th century, closed December 1989.
Wilton House, Old People's Home	Formerly Wilton House, private residence, 1880s. Later a club. Bombed. Present Home opened 16 May 1956.
Eastholme	1892.
Claremont, Elmhurst	Conjectured 1892 from style.
Carlton House	Between 1872 and 1884.
Beechwood Court	Early 1976.
Jehovah's Witness Hall	1958, site of Studley House.
Thornton Lodge and adjoining	There 1889.
No. 426, Mascarade	Post-World War 2 rebuild.
Nos. 428-432	Eastbourne Villas.
Gap	Formerly (1890-ish) part of Tattersall's nursery garden.
United Reformed Church	In 1890s houses.
Gap, Grandways car park	Site of houses, 1880s.
Grandways former fish shop	Fernleigh House, 1880s.
Post Office, No. 450	Beechwood House, 1880s.
Grandways extension	Fern Lodge (1880s) demolished for this in 1989.
Grandways	First phase of store.
Chemist, Raymond C. Hall, No. 464	Pine Wood Cottage.
Crown Inn (Mile House)	May have been an inn here for centuries. First evidence, 1748. 1938, inn demolished, present built.
Gap	Had been farm land (White House Farm).
Drill Hall	1913 hall demolished January 1990; new hall building, 1990.
Video shop, No. 506	Was Hull Co-op, built 1915.
Shops to corner, Nos. 508-518	There by 1911.
Brindley Street	About 1909.
Shops	1910-11.
Telford Street	About 1909.
Shops/houses	1910-11.
Kelvin Street	About 1907 started building.
Houses	There by 1908.
Faraday Street	About 1907 started building.

Houses	About 1910.
Lodge Street	Early 1930s.
2 shops	There by 1908.
Mill and cottages	There 1840, probably long before that. At one time occupied by Rank family, later Slater Eyre. 1989-90 converted to The Mill public house.
Baptist Church	1913; hall was first church, 1909.
Southcoates Avenue	About 1909.
Shops (purpose-built)	Formerly William Jackson and Son, about 1912.
Shops/houses	There by 1911.
Stanhope Avenue	1931-3.
Houses	There by 1911.
Kingsley Avenue	1931-3.
Houses/shops to Post Office, No. 706	Includes entrance to Craven Park, which was closed 1989; these houses pre-1908.
Wilkinson Avenue	There by 1933.
3 shops, Nos. 710-2-4	Pre-World War 1. No. 714 demolished 1990.
Gap	May, 1988. Leo's Supermarket, 1990.
Shops	
Aberdeen Street	1890s.
Filling Station	Site of St James' Parade.
Portobello Street	1890s.
Gap, car park	Site of Portobello Methodist Chapel built 1906, demolished 1984.
Portobello Chapel	Site of pre-1906 mission hall.
Houses — BOCM Village	About 1922.
Broadway	1922.
Houses to corner	About 1926-30.
Maybury Road	1925.
East-thorpe No. 800	Between 1898 and 1908.
Semi-detached houses Nos. 802-10	Built by 1908.
The Limes	Before 1908.
Greystones (Summerfield House)	
Ivanhoe (No. 824)	1938.
Filling station	On site of Glen Helen, private residence from early this century to after World War 2.
Kingston Wesley Chapel	1913.
Gap	Open space in front of Sperrin Close was Brunswick (Ferens') Recreation Ground.

Charnock Avenue	About 1979.
Semi-detached houses, Castleton, and 4 bungalows to No. 900	Between 1911 and 1920, not all same date.
Gap	Entrance to Schools' Playing Field.
St Michael's Church	Hall, 1913; Church 1927.
Marfleet Lane	There 1855, probably much earlier.
Houses to 934	1962, on site of Whitfield's farmstead, there 1852, probably much earlier.
Semi-detached houses Nos. 936-958	About 1908.
Bungalows	There in mid-1920s.
Detached House, No. 970	There in mid-1920s.
Scarcroft	On 1908 OS.
Semi-detached houses	Between World War 1 and 1925.
Irene Bungalows	Mid-1920s.
Holderness Drain	1832.
Ardmore Close	About 1970. [Named 1973]
No. 996, The Gables	Was there 1925, I think much earlier.
No. 998	On 1908 OS.
Semi-detached houses, Nos. 1000-30	On 1908 OS.
Block of 3 houses	Were called Eastholme Villas, pre-1908.
2 bungalows	Post-World War 2, perhaps mid-1950s.
The Haven	Built 1925.
Semi-detached houses	Between 1908 and 1920.
No. 1056 and 3 sets semis	On 1908 OS
Apollo Club and coach house	Late 1890s.
Diadem Grove	Early 1950s, there by 1955.
Trentholme and Wilfholme	Between 1908 and 1914.
Houses	About World War 1 or just after.
Thanet School	Originally Infants' 1955, Junior 1957.
Open ground	
Doctor's surgery	1989.
Fleet Estate	Late 1970s.

North side

Dansom Lane	In existence 1770, probably long before that.
Corner shops	1850.
Gap	Always there.
Twin buildings either side of Wilton Street	1850s.

The Humber Social Club in former bank premises at the end of Humber Terrace left complete after bombing. Holderness Road's single high-rise building, near Nornabell Street, is seen in the right background.

Wilton Street	1850s, included in 1851 census.
2 houses, round-headed windows	Late 1850s.
ex-Public Benefit	1890s.
No. 39, Whistling Kettle café	There 1861 as a house.
Crystal Ford car sales	1975, the site of Ellis's Terrace *etc.*
Studley Street	Started late 1860s.
Reckitt's Pharmaceutical	1979-80.
Beeton Street, now without name	A street by 1852. Last telegraph pole removed August 1989.
Mount Pleasant	1987-8.
Gap	Was Station Parade, shops, demolished 1987.
Courtney Street	Late 1850s, well populated by 1861.
Humber Terrace (complete)	1880s.
Adjoining terrace to Burleigh Street (7)	1880s.
Burleigh Street	About 1875.
Overhead bridge	1885.
Gap	World War 2 bombing.
Poplar Buildings	1880s.
Nornabell Street	About 1875.

Gap, was Argyle Buildings	World War 2 bombing.
Argyle Terrace (9 remaining of 10)	1880s.
Barnsley Street (was Garbutt Street)	About 1870, name changed by 1885.
Elephant and Castle	1872 a grocer's shop.
Albion Parade (6 remaining of 7)	1870s.
Gap, building in progress, 1990	World War 2 bombing.
Lorne Terrace	1870s.
Buckingham Street	About 1875.
Shops	1989, was Filey Parade, 1870s, bombed World War 2.
ex-Wm. Jackson & Sons Ltd	Early 1890s after closure of football
Severn Street, No. 317	ground.
Mersey Street, No. 319-327	Ditto
Shops between Severn and Mersey Streets	1990 on bombed site.
Brunswick	Schoolroom 1886, Chapel rebuilt 1962.
Shops to corner	There 1876.
Durham Street	On 1853 OS, but no houses until a year or two later.
Durham Villa (Bush, Optician)	There 1872, probably late 1860s.
Shops, Nos. 339-347	1880s, possibly earlier.
Shops with 'Dutch' gables (7)	1890s, except Nos. 357-9, rebuilt after World War 2 bombing.
Jalland Street	There 1889.
Chestnut Villas	Mid-1880s.
James Stuart Statue	1923.
Village Road	1908 as Chestnut Grove, name changed by 1914.
Holderness House	1838.
Laburnum Avenue	In 1850, a track; in 1889 called Jalland's Lane.
St. Columba's Church	1960 rebuild after 1943 bomb.
Parade of shops	1950s rebuild after bombing.
No. 425	End shop of original parade, between 1925 and 1930.
Westcott Street	1880s.
Westcott House, flats	1950s on site of Westcott House, home of Thomas Priestman, 1880s.
Wood Grange Residential Home	Home of Francis Reckitt, 1880s, sold for £1420 in 1913; later used by Christian Scientists.
Turnberry Court	1960s, I think.
Pink Panther Home	1893, former Drypool Vicarage.

Lee Street	In 1892 unnamed, no houses.
Burnbrae, The Cedars	Between 1901 and 1908.
St Mungo's	Between 1908 and 1914.
Summergangs Road	About 1911.
Shops	About 1911.
Park lodge	Soon after World War 2.
Toilets	About 1925.
East Park	This section opened 20 June 1887.
Park Lodge	1887.
Dance Hall	1939-40. Was Civil Defence Headquarters.
Woodford Centre	First phase opened 25 April 1982 by John Prestcott, M.P.
Houses/shops, East Park Avenue, Northguard, *etc.* Westminster Avenue, shops	Between 1901 and 1910, started by 1908.
Ferens Haven of Rest	1911, those behind, 1954.
Houses	1926.
Lake View	1926.
The Parade	1927.
Lake Drive	1927.
Astoria (originally a cinema)	1934.
Argyle Parade and The Willows	Between 1901 and 1908.
Houses, Nos. 697-709	Mid-1930s.
Tower Grange	Was there by 1895.
Hurley Close	Late 1960s.
Tower Grange Police Station	Operational from 1 April 1974, official opening 6 December 1974.
Church of Latter Day Saints	1965.
Washington, Wrenthorpe	About 1900.
The Laurels, Bel Carres	Soon after 1901.
Sunnydene, shops, Romany, Churchill House (formerly Baldwin House)	About 1900. Baldwin/Churchill House was East Hull Conservative Party Headquarters.
Carrick's corner	Site of Somergangs Toll Bar.
Ings Road	Probably even before the 18th century.
Crooked Billet	1966-7.
4 houses	Between 1914 and 1924.
Shops formerly Hull Co-op	1926.
Shaftesbury Avenue	Between 1912 and 1921.
Houses	First four, 1913; No. 831 Glaisdale or St Amant 1914, others later.
Bungalow	There by 1925.

Waldegrave Avenue	Between 1926 and 1930.
Houses	The Briers No. 853, 1912.
Ellesmere Avenue	Started 1912.
Houses and shops (Leyland Villas)	About 1912.
Block of 3 houses (Nos. 875-9)	Early 1930s.
Nos. 881-3	There by 1925.
Freshfield, St Helier, Calderstones	After 1925.
Nos. 891-3	There by 1925.
Corporation housing to Four-in-Hand	Replaced 1940s pre-fabs that were there until early 1970s.
Four-in-Hand	Present building 1937.
Bellfield Avenue	As Four Alls Lane, was there early last century, probably before. Bellfield Avenue houses begun 1930.
Corporation housing to drain	Further part of Ings Road estate, begun 1963.
Drain	1832 as Holderness Drain, formerly River Wilflete. Bridge part of 1950s road widening.
Corporation housing	
Nos. 1143-5	1936-7.
Nos. 1151-3	Post-World War 2.
Minster Court No. 1167	
Nos. 1169-1183	1930s. Terrington about 1937, St Louie 1935.
Nos. 1185-7	Post-World War 2.
*No. 1189, Eastfield House, John Parkin & Son, Funeral Directors	Original house 1680, altered and up-dated.
*No. 1191, Eastfield Cottage	Originally about 1600, much altered.
Saltshouse Road	Old road, perhaps before 18th century. Was Saltshouse Lane.
Longhill Estate	Between 1952 and 1959, Shannon Road opened in 1952.
Filling Station	Late 1950s, site of farm and Bilton Bridge.
Ganstead Lane	Another old road.
Swiss Cottage Hotel	About 1956-7, called the Ganstead until about 1984.

*Eastfield Cottage at No. 1191 and Eastfield House at No. 1189 (and also called 3, Saltshouse Road) are the oldest buildings left on Holderness Road, much older than the 1838 Holderness House.

UP TO NOW

The city boundary now crosses the main road at Waterworks Lane, Bilton, and the Asda store, but Holderness Road as such ends at the Ganstead roundabout.

It has become more difficult to consider the road in isolation as no longer is it a long and narrow but single entity. The side streets now form an intermeshing web with streets from other main roads and 'the Holderness Road area' is not defined as simply as it used to be when streets finished in fields at the ends away from the main road. Building after the war in this part of Hull was largely Corporation housing and, instead of individual streets, there were the extensive estates. Longhill came early: it was started in 1952 and finished by 1959. During the same period, although it did not take so long, Holderness Road was modernised from Summergangs Road outwards, the first part of that task made easier because of the established dual carriageway formed by the roads on each side of the old tram track.

The poplar trees lining the tracks were removed, the rails had gone when the trolleys came and the centre area became the reservation of shrubs, flowers and small trees that we have today. Beyond Ings Road, there had to be some widening, with more disruption to the north side than the south, as ancient hedgerows were rooted out, ditches filled and gardens shortened. A better road eased the problem of construction traffic for the Holderness Road estates. Longhill and Bilton Grange were building together; Thanet's first school opened in 1955 and East Mount on Longhill in January 1957.

Two small estates which have apparently escaped some of the problems of the larger ones were built, one on land north of the drain between Saltshouse and Holderness Road, East Mount Avenue running through this one, and another east of Bellfield Avenue. Both of these are quiet and well-kept with more of the feeling of a privately-owned estate of houses. The prefabs opposite Marfleet Lane were taken down in the early '70s, when Ings Road Estate gradually spread up to Sutton.

Building these estates removed the farmsteads which had been in the district for more than a century, some of them, I suspect, for nearer two hundred years. Wray's beyond the drain bridge and Wright's just before it, the farm yard at the corner of Saltshouse Road and at Bilton Bridge, as well as two rural houses near the Four-in-Hand, were suddenly gone and, the new road being without hedgerows and ditches, the area beyond Ings Road had suddenly become urban.

One night in about 1960 the kingpost of the farm at the corner of Marfleet Lane gave way and the roof fell in. The house was still occupied, but no-one was hurt. The farm and all its outbuildings were cleared and the trees cut down — and there was a prime building site. Fortunately it escaped becoming a petrol station and, instead, two rows of houses designed by Alan Plater were built by McCollins on Holderness Road and in Marfleet Lane in 1962. Then the removal of Fussey's farm from Ings Road corner, followed by the building of the Crooked Billet in the mid-Sixties, really swept away the last vestiges of the rural nature of Holderness Road 'beyond the tram ends'.

Linking East Hull with other parts of the city had already been accomplished with the inner and outer ring roads. Sutton Road bridge gave a much higher river crossing away from the main water traffic and, although it is an opening bridge, it does not provide the regular high tide barrier to road traffic as North Bridge does. In the mid-Fifties Sutton Road was truly a ring road, well outside the built-up area. Few people think of the Laburnum Avenue, Chamberlain Road, Clough Road route as the Inner Ring Road today as it is now comparatively close to the centre, but it was the construction of link roads such as these which opened up building possibilities and to some extent lessened the importance of the radial roads. However, the increase in the number of vehicles soon clogged these cross-links and the most recent solution, indirectly made possible by the war, has been the late 1980s' opening of Mount Pleasant, using the line of the old railway to link Stoneferry with Hedon Road and ultimately with the motorway.

Holderness Road as a market has therefore shrunk; the shopping area is now from Southcoates Lane to the overhead bridge, with Grandways and the shops opposite the park gates as a group on their own. More shopping is done by car, more men help with domestic shopping, and the task is further altered by the supermarkets which are now the chains jostling for main road positions. Asda opened on the periphery of the city in 1982 and serves people from country villages as well as parts of East Hull. Grandways is popular with foot-and-bus shoppers and also those with cars, but at the moment the Co-op is aiming to provide fresh competition with the opening in autumn 1990 of Leo's on Craven Park. This will alter shopping patterns and it remains to be seen what will happen to the smaller shops of the Parade and round about, which have been useful all-round providers for 60-odd years.

There was a time when it was remarked that Holderness Road had 'lost its guts', but the area of the main shop density has revived in recent years, becoming lively with new shops and a good range of merchandise. Behind the shops, relatively new, lower density housing than the old terraces provides many of the customers. The traffic which could divide one side of the road from the other as by a wall, is controlled by a lot of Pelican crossings and, although the south side is generally more popular, it is fairly easy to cross the road. Here the pedestrian has been catered for.

Because of the trees surrounding Holderness House, as well as those at the roadside, Holderness Road from Jalland Street retains a little of the gracious air it had at the turn of the century. Small trees in the central reservation from Mile House are maturing and the park gates are still overshadowed by the chestnuts. Many elm trees have died, so that the statue of James Stuart, put there by Mr Ferens because he so admired the work Stuart had done for the city, is no longer overshadowed and stands proud. The older larger houses beyond Ings Road and near Westcott Street have become homes for the elderly. The oldest houses down in Wilton Terrace are barely recognisable, but here and there, at Nos. 31 and 33, for example, and above the shops of East Parade one can glimpse the former homes of middle-class go-ahead tradespeople who made Holderness Road — and Hull — what it became.

At the Witham end of the road is a reminder that last century people walked. In the spandrels of the ornamented front of what used to be the Public Benefit shop (opposite the Green Man) one can still see what was sold there: boots. Out-of-the-ordinary things like this are missed when they go, but sometimes barely noticed when they are there. It was a sad day at the end of May 1988 when the tramsheds' facade was pulled down, suddenly and without warning. The old nursery greenhouse that was Darling's greengrocery and florist's shop opposite the Holderness House Lodge was also missed. People like variety, new and old together, brick and stone, brash and restrained, yellow and blue. This is all there on Holderness Road, the very mixture making it ordinary and unique at the same time.

I have tried to bring together some facts so that the memory of events personal to a reader may be more accurately aroused. Out of all the 'characters' on the road, one stands out in my mind: that was Henry on the trams and trolley-buses, he of the thick spectacles and cheery catch-phrase, 'Anybody want to pay?' as he came for the fares. I think, too, that a whole generation of people will recall the sick man who lay at the window of one of the houses in Wilton Terrace and who became so well-known that he was accorded a greater recognition in the *Hull Daily Mail* at his passing than others of more distinction in the city.

However, this cannot be the complete story of Holderness Road to the present time as such an epic would be made up of the lives of thousands. Names mentioned will strike chords here and there. To find out more, the Local Studies Library in Albion Street has the material for further research. To those who take up a study like this: I hope that they will also meet as many people as I did who tell of people and places, giving vital clues to the next step forward; that their friends will be forebearing, as once started, this kind of research becomes absorbing; and, finally, I know from grateful experience that at the Local Studies Library every visitor from the timid amateur to the accomplished historian receives the same interested, willing and courteous service from Miss Jill Crowther and her staff. Thanks are also due to the Secretary of Hull Trinity House, the Archivist of Rank Hovis McDougall, the *Hull Daily Mail* and Humberside Leisure Services. I am grateful too to Mr. Michael Wilson for drawing the map of Holderness Road. To the acquaintances, friends and librarians, my deep gratitude: some of the impetus came from them, all mistakes and omissions are my own.

To find out more, you could consult, among others:

K. J. Allison (ed.), *A History of the County of York East Riding Volume I: The City of Kingston upon Hull* (1969).
Thomas Blashill, *Evidences Relating to East Hull* (Hull, 1903).
E. Wrigglesworth, *Brown's Illustrated Guide to Hull* (Hull, 1891).
K. A. MacMahon, *Roads and Turnpike Trusts in Eastern Yorkshire*, East Yorkshire Local History Series, No. 18 (York, 1964).
M. E. Ingram, *Drypool* (Gloucester, 1959).
J. Markham, *Streets of Hull* (Beverley, 1987).
C. A. Foster, *Court Housing in Kingston-upon-Hull*, University of Hull Occasional Papers in Geography, No. 19 (Hull, 1972).
J. O'Hara, *Men of the City* (Hull, 1914).
Hull and East Riding Red Books (Hull, 1898, 1899, 1900).
H. J. Whiting, *Portraits of Public Men* (Hull, 1858).
Issued by Joseph Rank Ltd. *The Master Millers*, (1955).
S. Marshall, *History of Co-operative Development (Hull & District)* (Manchester, 1951).
Hull Anti-Mill Society Rules (Hull, 1856). [Hull Local Studies Library].
R. F. Drewery, *History of Methodism in Hull* (Hull, 1974). [Typescript].
Mrs. J. Garbutt, *Reminiscences of the early days of Primitive Methodism in Hull* (1886).
K. Hoole, *Regional History of the Railways of Great Britain* (Newton Abbot, 1986).
Kingston-upon-Hull Museums, *Hull Tramways, the early days* (Lockington, 1977).
J. S. Nicholson, *The Tramways of Kingston-upon-Hull*, in Tramway Museum Society, Trams, No. 27, October 1967 and No. 28, January 1968.
M. E. Ulyatt, *Hull Kingston Rovers R.L.F.C., A Centenary History, 1883-1983* (Lockington, 1983).
Malet Lambert Local History Reprint, No. 27, *The Garden Village*, 1913, reprinted 1982 by permission of the Garden Village Society, Hon. Sec., Mr Walter Houlton.
Lutyens and Abercrombie, *A Plan for the City & County of Kingston upon Hull* (Hull, 1945).
and very many directories, Burgess Rolls, newspapers, maps and handbooks of various organisations. Lots of walking with eyes open yields a different picture from that obtained by swift passage in bus or car, observation being an essential adjunct to the books.